ANTIPASTI

Library of Congress Cataloging-in-Publication Data
Della Croce, Julia,
        [Antipasti]
        antipasti : the little dishes of italy / by
Julia della Croce ; Photography by Joyce
Oudkerk Pool.
            p.   cm.
        ISBN #0-8118-0697-9
        ISBN #0-8118-0218-3 (pb)
        1.Appetizers. 2.Cookery, Italian. I.Title.
    TX740.D465 1993
    641.8'12–dc20   92-34462
                                        CIP

Printed in Japan

Cover and interior design by
Aufuldish & Warinner
Editing by Sharon Silva
Food styling by Amy Nathan

Distributed in Canada by Raincoast Books,
112 East Third Ave., Vancouver, B.C. V5T 1C8

10 9 8 7 6 5 4 3 2

Chronicle Books
275 Fifth Street
San Francisco, CA
94103

THE LITTLE DISHES OF ITALY

ANTIPASTI

JULIA DELLA CROCE

PHOTOGRAPHY BY JOYCE OUDKERK POOL

FOOD STYLING BY AMY NATHAN

CHRONICLE BOOKS

SAN FRANCISCO

CONTENTS

✳

ACKNOWLEDGMENTS

❊

Above all, thanks go to my husband, Bob Stien, and to my children, Gabriella and Celina, even if they do not like vegetables. Without my family, eating is a lonely joy. They are the anchor without which my gastronomical ship would float aimlessly. I thank them also for enduring my absences during my intense work periods, and for supporting me and sustaining me. ❊ Then, to my mother, Giustina Ghisu della Croce, whose infallible sense of taste outshines anyone else's. She is always at my side in the kitchen, even when she is not literally there. ❊ To Alex Barakov, for his extraordinary devotion to my family during my absences, not only tending my children, but keeping my house in order. ❊ To Peter Susser, for putting his cellist's ear to my text, which improved it, and his vigorous appetite to the recipes herein, especially the vegetable ones. ❊ To Dean Sharenow, for his computer wizardry, without which I would still be typing. ❊ To Anna Amendolara Nurse, *mia seconda mamma,* for her kindness and generosity in sharing her knowledge of Italian cooking, and for her recipe contributions. ❊ To my friend Flavia Destefanis, for all her research help, and for the loving eye with which she looked over my manuscript. ❊ To Anita Katz, my friend, for she has touched this book in many ways. ❊ To my agent, Judith Weber, who always does far more than any agent could be expected to, for guiding me in this project. ❊ To Nancy Q. Keefe, whom I can never thank enough for leading me to my first newspaper job. It led me to this work I love. ❊ To Bill LeBlond, my editor, for his faith in my work, and to my associates at Chronicle Books, who give me the opportunity to make my books beautiful; to Mary Ann Gilderbloom, my publicity director, for her unflagging enthusiasm. ❊ To Sharon Silva, for her painstaking attention to every detail of the text of this book so that it would be as clear and useful to readers as it could be, and with especial gratitude for her understanding of Italian cooking. ❊ To Amy Nathan, whose remarkable eye for food styling and exquisite taste make the photographs so beguiling, and to Joyce Oudkerk Pool, whose stunning photography brings this food to life. ❊ To Lisa and Lou Ekus, extraordinary publicists and remarkable human beings, who have done so much to advance my work. ❊ I also owe a debt to numerous cookbooks from which I have gained a greater understanding of Italian food, and of *antipasti* in particular. Foremost among these are Ada Boni's *Talismano della felicità,* Pellegrino Artusi's *La scienza in cucina e l'arte di mangiar bene,* Marcella Hazan's *The Classic Italian Cookbook,* Waverley Root's *The Food of Italy,* Anna Del Conte's *Gastronomy of Italy,* Massimo Alberini and Giorgio Mistretta's *Guida all'Italia gastronomica,* and Elizabeth David's *Italian Food,* which is always inspirational, no matter how many times I reread it. In addition, I am grateful to Lidia Bastianich, *Gourmet* magazine, and to The American Institute of Wine and Food for sponsoring the Italian Pantry lectures, from which I learned more than I already knew about Italian ingredients that are essential to the *antipasto* table. ❊ To all those named here, and to all those contributors mentioned in the recipes, I express my gratitude and thanks.

INTRODUCTION

ANTIPASTI

THE LITTLE DISHES OF ITALY

EVERY cookbook writer hopes to lure readers beyond the covers of her book, to beguile them by the tastes, colors, and aromas of the dishes inside. I hope to do that by drawing you into the Italian way of eating. It is a simple style that reflects the landscape, history, and traditions of a colorful and exuberant people, one that has ancient roots and that is still, gratefully, practiced much the way it has been for hundreds of years. Of course, Italian cooking has not been impervious to modern influences. Cuisine, like culture, is living, influenced by the forces of history and social change.

❋ The category of *antipasti* is perhaps the most modern aspect of the Italian table. These little dishes have traditionally been presented at restaurants, on holidays, and at weddings, buffets, formal dinners, and the like. This extra course before the meal has typically been a part of the daily eating habits of wealthier households rather than that of peasant abodes, where traditions center around home cooking. Except for *affettati*, delicious cured sliced meats including tongue, *prosciutto*, *salame*, dried sausages, and other local specialties, *antipasti* are not usually part of the family dinner.

❋ Surely one change connected with the passing of the vigorous rural lifestyles of many Italians is that, on the whole, the nation eats lighter and less. This change is evident in the comparison of Italian cookbooks written a century ago, or even fifty years ago, with those written today. The traditional large midday meal is fast becoming a thing of the past in many parts of Italy, as women go outside the home to work and more families abandon the countryside to join the ranks of city workers. Many Italians now eat more simply on a break from the office, or even at home, because other family members are no longer present. Where there was once time for a lengthy *pranzo* beginning with an assortment of locally produced *salumi* ("cold cuts"), lunch or supper might now more often consist of a *frittata* of zucchini, peppers, artichokes, or whatever, accompanied with vegetables or other light dishes, or a *spaghettata*, a meal consisting solely of pasta. Dishes that were once considered starters or *intermezzi* are now more frequently eaten as a meal.

❋ In Italian, the word *antipasto* means, literally, "before the meal." To most Americans, the word conjures images of a cold platter of *salame*, olives, pickled vegetables, and perhaps an Italian cheese or two served as an appetizer in an American-Italian restaurant. But in Italy, *antipasti* are not perfunctory beginnings to dinner; neither are they mere collections of cold meats and preserved vegetables. Rather, *antipasti* can be among the most creative dishes in the Italian kitchen, their variety endless, the assortment delectable. And while it is true that a delicious selection of *affet-*

tati, local olives, cheeses, and such are ubiquitous starters all over Italy, *antipasti* come in many forms: savory breads and pies, *crostini* ("little toasts") with all kinds of toppings, fish and shellfish, meat, vegetable, bean, *polenta*, rice, and salad dishes, both hot and cold.

❉ In *The Classic Italian Cookbook*, Marcella Hazan rightly describes *antipasti* as "the rogues of the Italian table." For not only are they enticing to look at and seductively delicious, but also they play many roles. For example, *cima alla genovese*, braised breast of veal stuffed with ground meats, sausage, pistachios, herbs, and eggs, is considered a starter to a meal and at other times the meal itself. What is sometimes a *contorno*, a side dish of vegetables served with or after the main course, might appear on the *antipasto* table as well. Or an *antipasto* might comprise, either alone or in combination with other starters, a whole meal.

❉ Anyone who has traveled to Italy is no doubt familiar with the fare of the *rosticceria*, where many *antipasti* are sold for take-out. Just before mealtimes these establishments are always full of people buying precooked dishes to carry home. But this is hardly fast food as we know it. Everything is freshly made, and the assortment is astonishing: roasted or poached meats stuffed with ham, cheese, and spinach, or with a *frittata*; whole mushrooms marinated in extra-virgin olive oil and herbs; all manner of meat, potato, and rice croquettes; salads of everything from poached artichoke hearts to grilled eggplant. There seems to be no limit to the creativity of these preparations.

❉ The repertoire of *antipasto* salads alone that qualifies is dazzling: rice salads brimming with shrimp, pine nuts, and strips of sweet ham; poached fresh peas tossed with almonds and mint; seafood salads of tender squid, shrimp, poached fish, clams, and other shellfish dressed with glistening green extra-virgin olive oil and lemon.

❉ *Focaccia, pizzelle* (little pizzas), *frittelle,* and other savory breads and farinaceous delicacies comprise another type of *antipasto.* Each can be eaten with a meal, for a snack, or on its own for a light (and portable) breakfast, lunch, or supper. The variations here, too, are many and marvelous.

❉ Because *antipasti* lend themselves to advance preparation, they are ideal for entertaining. Of all the spectacular dishes Italians prepare, perhaps none are so inviting as numerous *antipasti* in great and splendid array at a buffet. It is customary to encounter this bountiful assortment spread out enticingly on a long, polished marble counter or otherwise elegantly appointed table just inside the entrance of restaurants throughout Italy.

❉ Most of these dishes can be prepared here, for not only is it now possible to buy almost any Italian product in America, from extra-virgin olive oil to authentic *prosciutto* from Parma, but most *antipasti* require nothing more than fresh ingredients. Vegetables in particular are the foundation of many tasty and healthful *antipasti*. Sometimes they are offered raw: thin, crisp slices of fresh, sweet fennel served with lemon, fruity olive oil, and a veil of freshly ground pepper. Sometimes they are cooked: small, tender zucchini sliced very thin, layered with slices of tomato, fresh *mozzarella, parmigiano,* and shredded basil, covered with beaten eggs, and baked into a "pie" to be eaten hot or cold.

❉ Most important of all the ingredients on the *antipasto* table is olive oil. Aromatic extra-virgin olive oil transforms the barest ingredient into a finished dish. *Bruschetta* is nothing more than toasted peasant bread rubbed with a clove of garlic and drizzled with this fruity oil. The flavor of a plate of boiled beans or vegetables is instantly heightened by the addition of extra-virgin olive oil. Boiled *baccalà* ("salt cod") becomes an immensely appealing dish with a scattering of roughly chopped parsley and a dressing of fragrant olive oil.

❋ The lightness, simplicity, and flexibility of many of these dishes fit in perfectly with the hurried and health-conscious American life-style. They are the Italian answer to fast food, but more appetizing and elegant and infinitely more healthful. I say this knowing how cooking "Italian" has revolutionized the lives of people I know. For several years, I entertained friends and ran dining cruises on board a fifty-foot ketch on Long Island Sound. Because I cooked Italian dishes, I was able to work with the restrictions of a tiny galley kitchen, an alcohol stove with only two burners, and an ice chest (no refrigerator). An *antipasto* dish I made often was a Tuscan salad of *cannellini* beans, tinned Italian tuna, and finely sliced red onion or scallions, moistened with a peppery dressing of fruity olive oil and lemon juice. Boiled vegetables of all kinds—beets, green beans, cauliflower, broccoli, and zucchini, just to name the most common—anointed with the same dressing were other *antipasto* standbys. Poached fresh fish drizzled with this dressing and scattered with chopped fresh parsley was also a dish I served regularly. People have loved these simple, tasty recipes, and many friends have included them in their own repertoires of quick starter dishes or light luncheon fare.

❋ All Italian cooking is characterized by a reverence for fresh ingredients, simple preparation, and harmonious combinations of ingredients that bring out, rather than disguise the flavors of foods. It could be argued that *antipasti* are the most versatile and appealing of all Italian dishes.

The sources for my recipes are numerous. They have come from my experiences of traveling and staying in Italy from the time I was a young girl, from the way my family has always done things, and from the way I have seen things done in the homes of my mother's relations who are all, somehow, extraordinary cooks. A few are from Italian friends whose cooking I have found to be irresistible, and a few others are begged from restaurants whose dishes I found particularly good. But many are my own personal adaptations and interpretations of classic recipes or food combinations and, as such, present a very personal interpretation of the *antipasto* table.

❋ The yields for all the recipes in this book are designed for the *antipasto* course, which on the Italian table precedes the first course of pasta, *risotto*, or soup. But as I have said, many of these dishes can be eaten as main courses, *contorni*, or snacks. Readers will want to adjust recipe yields accordingly for larger portions.

CHAPTER 1

ESSENTIAL
INGREDIENTS

❋❋❋

ONLY the freshest and the best ingredients are used in the cooking of Italy. The aim is for the finished product to taste clearly of itself, even after cooking. The flavors of the ingredients should not be masked by complex sauces and discordant seasonings. The brilliance of Italian cooks is in their ability to enhance the natural flavors of fresh foods by combining them with the most carefully handcrafted local ingredients (olive oil, cheese, *prosciutto*) without radically transforming them. ❋ It would not be enough to set forth my prescriptions for appetizers without writing a chapter on the first steps. Recipes are only as good as the raw materials from which they are composed. Quality ingredients are crucial to the success of any dish. There is no rule so straightforward and so absolute as this when it comes to Italian cooking. The second axiom, if an empirical term can be applied to such a lively art, is to combine ingredients that complement one another. Only true love will make for a felicitous marriage. And so it is in cooking. The elements in a dish must be like lovers who cannot resist each other. ❋ An understanding of the nature of ingredients is critical to mastery in the kitchen. To appreciate and make full use of what Italian specialty foods are now available in America, I have elaborated on the cheeses and *salumi* (*prosciutto, mortadella, salame*), for they can be served on the antipasto table without any preparation. As for olive oil, Italian vinegars, mushrooms, and other staples of the Italian pantry, all of these are now widely stocked in specialty-food shops and even some supermarkets in America.

ANCHOVIES, in Italian, *acciughe.* In general, the American palate is not comfortable with the taste and texture of anchovies. I find that more people eschew them than almost any other food in the Italian cupboard. But as well as being delicious in salads and various cold *antipasti,* they are immensely useful when cooked with other ingredients. When heated, they disintegrate and virtually transform sauces and cooked dishes, adding flavor and saltiness. ❋ Anchovies are preserved in two ways: salted dry, or packed in olive oil in cans or bottles. Anchovies packed in salt are sold in large cans, so they are somewhat impractical for the home

5		12	
ACCIUGHE anchovies		**OLIVE** olives	
6		12	
FAGIOLI beans		**OLIO DI OLIVA** olive oil	
6		14	
PANE GRATTUGIATO bread crumbs		**PINOLI** pine nuts	
7		14	
CAPPERI capers		**POMODORI** tomatoes	
7		14	
FORMAGGI cheeses		**POMODORI SECCHI** sun-dried tomatoes	
10		15	
SALUMI cold cuts		**TONNO SOTT'OLIO** tuna	
11		15	
FUNGHI mushrooms		**ACETO** vinegar	

kitchen. They should always be rinsed and then filleted before use, or their saltiness will be excessive. Once a can or bottle has been opened, the anchovies can be kept in the refrigerator for several weeks, although their saltiness will deepen. Store either type of preserved anchovies immersed in olive oil in a tightly closed glass jar. When a recipe calls for only a few anchovies, anchovy paste is an option, although its flavor is less intense than that of preserved fillets.

BEANS, in Italian, *fagioli.* Now and then I find shell beans in American markets, but such discoveries are rare. Therefore, the recipes offered in this book call for dried beans and lentils. This is not a sacrifice of quality, however, for dried beans are an excellent product. Rehydrating dried beans takes more time than opening a can, but I feel that the resulting firm texture of the beans makes the preparation worthwhile.

Canned beans can be used in a pinch; just remember that their texture is very soft, so if they are cooked too long, they will fall apart. For bean salads, rinse canned beans with cold water and drain them thoroughly before dressing them. In recipes for cooked beans, add them only for the last ten minutes of cooking and reduce the salt in the recipe to compensate for the canned beans' higher salt content. Canned chick-peas remain firmer than other kinds of canned beans, so do not hesitate to substitute them for dried chick-peas.

When stored for too long, dried beans can become excessively hard, and even lengthy presoaking will not rehydrate them sufficiently. Wrinkled skin is a sign that they are too hard. It is wise to use dried beans within a year of purchase.

To rehydrate beans, put them in a large bowl with cold water to cover by three inches. Let them stand for a minimum of four hours, or as long as overnight at room temperature. Drain them and they are ready to be cooked. An alternative method is to put them in a large saucepan with water to cover by three inches.

Bring them to a boil, cover, and remove them from the heat. Let them stand for one hour, then drain and proceed with the cooking.

Beans are highly nutritious. When cooked, they contain from 210 to 240 calories per one-cup serving, and many of these calories are burned up during digestion. In fact, proportionally more calories are required to digest beans than most other foods. Beans provide dietary fiber, which aids in digestion and colon functions. According to some scientific studies, beans contribute to the prevention of colon cancer. They contain from 2 to 6 percent fat and no cholesterol. Beans are nearly complete in protein; combined with small amounts of animal protein or dairy products, they fulfill the daily human requirement for protein, plus they contain many vitamins and minerals.

BREAD CRUMBS, in Italian, *pane grattugiato* or *pane grattato.* Dried bread crumbs have many roles in the Italian kitchen. They are used to thicken sauces such as *salsa rossa* (an uncooked tomato sauce served with boiled meats), *salsa verde* (a piquant parsley sauce for meats and fish), and brothy seafood sauces; to coat sautéed and deep-fried foods; and to top baked dishes to form a crisp crust. They are also sprinkled onto greased pan surfaces for such dishes as *sformati* (molded dishes of rice, pasta, or whatever) to enable them to be easily unmolded. Fresh rather than dried bread crumbs are sometimes combined with other ingredients for stuffings, in *polpettone* ("meatloaf"), and *polpette* (poached or fried "meatballs").

Canned dried bread crumbs, especially those marked "Italian bread crumbs," often contain dried parsley, onion, monosodium glutamate, and other ingredients that are heretical to fine cooking. Only pure bread crumbs–those without flavorings or other ingredients–are suitable.

Hard bread can be easily pulverized in a food processor or blender or with a hand grater. Use dense (not airy) Italian or other white so-called peasant bread containing no sugar, herbs, or flavorings. Break it up into small pieces before toasting and grinding. Keep the crumbs in a closed glass jar or container in the pantry. Bread absorbs moisture, so it is important to keep crumbs in a dry place–never in the refrigerator. Unless the recipe directs otherwise, toast them lightly before using to prevent them from absorbing oil too easily. The easiest way to do this is in a heavy skillet over medium heat. Stir the crumbs occasionally with a wooden spoon in order to toast them evenly.

CAPERS, in Italian, *capperi*. Capers are the salted or pickled flower buds of the caper plant (*Capparis spinosa*), which grows wild in the Mediterranean and in India. The finest capers are the smallest, tightest, tulip-shaped ones. They are picked by hand before sunrise, when the flowers have not had a chance to open to the light or be wilted by the heat, then they are allowed to rest in the dark for several hours before pickling.

Nasturtium buds are often passed off as capers, but lack the firm texture and peppery taste of true capers. In Italy, capers are most often salted and sold by weight; they must be rinsed with cold water before they are used. Here, capers are more commonly available preserved in brine; they do not need rinsing.

CHEESES, in Italian, *formaggi*. According to the Italian Cheese Consortium, there are 450 different cheeses produced in Italy. Italian cheeses are made by people, not through a highly industrialized and impersonal factory process. Each cheese is a unique product reflecting local customs and traditions, and influenced by historical, sociological, and geographical factors. On the Italian table, cheeses are served both before the meal, as *antipasti,* and after, with fruit. Some of them are suitable for use in cooking.

❋ **MOZZARELLA** is a fresh, soft cheese, so it is best eaten when it is dripping wet, the same day it is made. True *mozzarella* is made from the milk of the water buffalo, but is seldom exported to this country because it sours rapidly. Cow's milk *mozzarella* is called *fior di latte*, or "flower of milk." Many Italian specialty shops in America make their own cow's milk *mozzarella* daily. The creamy-white braids and fists of cheese, which can usually be seen bathing in water in large stainless-steel pans or in huge glass jars on the countertops, are often offered in both salted and salt-free varieties. The latter, an American phenomenon, is virtually tasteless, however. A bland cheese, *mozzarella* nonetheless has an unqualified charm. It is often marinated in extra-virgin olive oil for the *antipasto* table and served with olives. A typical Neapolitan *antipasto* that has many regional variations is *mozzarella in carrozza* ("in a carriage"), in which the cheese is sandwiched between slices of bread, dipped into beaten egg, soaked for some thirty minutes, and deep-fried.

❋ **GRANA,** or *grana padano*, is a category of cheese produced in the Po Valley, parts of Piedmont, Lombardy, Veneto, and Emilia-Romagna. The prized *parmigiano-reggiano* (see below) is one of its members. *Grana* is produced in larger quantities outside the five famous cheese-producing provinces. Aged six months less than *parmigiano*, it is not as creamy or complex in taste as its more noble cousin. Young *grana* is a good table cheese, although not on par with authentic *parmigiano*, while aged *grana* is more suitable for grating. The markings on the cheese rind tell you whether it is *parmigiano-reggiano* or *grana*.

❋ **PARMIGIANO-REGGIANO** is the most famous and most precious Italian table cheese, with seven hundred years of cheese-making tradition behind it. The soil, climate, air, vegetation, and cattle-raising traditions of five provinces–all of Parma, Reggio Emilia, and Modena, as well as Mantua on the right bank of the Po River, and Bologna on the left bank of the Reno River–are essential to the success of this cheese, as is the craft of those producing it. While *parmigiano-reggiano* has many pretenders, the authentic cheese is produced in only these five provinces. Made from cow's milk produced in the spring, it takes about 150 gallons of milk to make a fifty-pound wheel. The wheels are then aged for eighteen months to four years, during which time the flavor and saltiness of the cheese intensify. *Parmigiano* that is aged for more than two years is termed *stravecchio*. The year of production is clearly marked in the stamp that is branded into the crust of the cheese. The *parmigiano*-making process is completely natural, with no affirmatives used in the milk or the rennet. The result is an inimitable cheese that is expensive to buy, even in Italy.

This is an extraordinary eating cheese that is indispensable on the *antipasto* table, but it is also a cooking cheese. When cooking with it, remember that the less heat to which it is exposed, the better, for heat damages the complex flavor. This is especially true of the more aged cheeses. If the cheese becomes stringy when heated, it is too young for cooking. When adding it to soups, *risotti*, or pasta, sprinkle it on at the last minute.

Master cheesemonger Steve Jenkins, who has personally introduced numerous Italian cheeses in America, points out that it is the only cheese that has a whole school of cuisine behind it, that of authentic northern Italian cooking. The best *parmigiano* is a rich, warm straw color and has an intense flavor and fragrance. It has a granular "biting" texture, firm and flaky, yet moist, with no holes in it. Never use the pregrated, bottled or canned cheeses sold as *parmigiano* and called "Parmesan" or "Italian-style grating cheese." These are not *parmigiano* and have little merit. A simple rule of thumb offered by the *parmigiano* producers should guide you when buying: the cheese must be two years old for the table, three years old for topping pasta dishes, and four years old for *tortellini* fillings.

❋ **PECORINO** is cheese made from sheep's milk. These cheeses are produced in all stages of maturity, from very soft (*pecorino fresco*, "fresh") to hard, aged varieties (*pecorino stagionato*). *Pecorino* is the oldest known Italian cheese. Today, some type of *pecorino* is made in every Italian region, although it is more typi-

cal of the poorer Italian south, where fewer cattle are raised than in the verdant north.

While the techniques for making these cheeses are relatively primitive in comparison to those employed in the production of *parmigiano-reggiano* and other northern Italian cheeses, young *pecorino* (not older than three months) is good for the *antipasto* table. The aged varieties are compatible with southern Italian dishes, which are characteristically bolder in flavor than the refined cooking of the northern table. What is exported to America are the harder varieties from Lazio (of which Rome is the capital city) and Sardinia, and an excellent semisoft sheep cheese from Umbria and Tuscany, called caciotta in this country. *Pecorino romano* is probably the best sheep's milk cheese exported here, although *caciotta di Siena* can often be found in well-stocked cheese markets. *Fiordi Sardegna*, a semisoft Sardinian sheep cheese useful in southern Italian cooking, is exported in small quantities. But remember, these are saltier, sharper, and less rounded than *parmigiano-reggiano* or grana, and should not be substituted for them.

❋ **FONTINA,** a Piedmontese cheese with a history of five hundred years behind it, is made with great skill and care. A semisoft, nutty, somewhat sweet cheese made from cow's milk, fontina has many uses on the *antipasto* table. It is a good cheese for melting onto *crostini di polenta* (page 102), for baking with mushrooms and other vegetables, and for many other cooking purposes. In Piedmont, it is combined with sweet butter and white truffles for canapés. And, of course, it is the cheese that goes into the famous Piedmontese *fonduta* (page 48).

❋ **GORGONZOLA** has generated many legends describing its origin. One of the most popular is that it was discovered in the ninth century when Lombardian shepherds left a cheese to ripen in a damp cave and found a pleasant-tasting mold growing on it. The cheese makers say that this very same mold is added to rich fresh cheese today to enable it to ferment. Made from cow's milk and cow's rennet, creamy *gorgonzola* is considered one of the world's most unique cheeses. It is characterized by the blue green veins that run through it and by its pungent, barnyard aroma. Young *gorgonzola* is relatively mild, creamy and sweet. As it ages, it becomes *piccante*, spicy and very strong. Among its uses on the *antipasto* table are on canapés, mixed with butter for spreading on *crostini*, used as a topping for *focaccia*, and baked into puff pastry. Like other perishable fresh cheeses, *gorgonzola* should be eaten within a day or two of purchase.

❈ **RICOTTA** (literally, "recooked") is a fresh cheese made from the whey that separates from the curd when heat is applied in the cheese-making process. The whey is reheated ("recooked") to form the fresh, soft cheese we call *ricotta*. In Italy, *ricotta* is produced from cow, goat, or ewe's milk, but in America it is made strictly from cow's milk. Americans are most familiar with its use in baked pasta dishes such as southern Italian–style *lasagne*, or as a filling for large pasta shapes such as shells. It can be made into soufflés, puddings, cakes, and pies, or eaten plain with or without sugar. On the *antipasto* table, *ricotta* is useful in vegetable stuffings such as that for *involtini di zucchine* (page 22) or as a filling for *crespelle* (*crêpes*). American *ricotta* is much looser than Italian ricotta, so when using it for fillings, it must be placed in a sieve for an hour or longer to drain and solidify.

❈ **RICOTTA SALATA** ("salted ricotta") is a creamy, slightly salty, tangy, soft but solid cheese made from *ricotta*. This simple, rustic cheese has become popular in America. Serve it with sharp-flavored black olives for an *antipasto*.

❈ **ROBBIOLA PIEMONTESE** can be made from cow, sheep, or goat's milk. It is very flavorful and delicate, with a slightly bitter taste that is part of its appeal. *Robbiola* is a fine table cheese. In some parts of Piedmont, the cheese is preserved in hermetically sealed glass jars with extra-virgin olive oil and aromatic herbs, a procedure that can easily be done at home.

❈ **TALEGGIO** is a soft, rich, buttery cow's milk cheese made in the mountain area of Bergamo, in Lombardy. It can be eaten crust and all. By law, it must be made from the milk of local cows. In its native area, *taleggio* is eaten with fruit after meals, but it is a fine cheese for the *antipasto* table.

❈ **TOMA,** literally a "hunk" or "round," is an unfermented cheese made from cow's milk, or a combination of milks, that is aged at least three months. It resembles Brie, but it should not be runny. There are varieties of toma ranging from mild to *piccante*, all with great flavor. *Toma* is a fine table cheese.

❈ **STORING AND SERVING CHEESES.** Cheeses are living, and so they perish quickly. They are best eaten as soon as possible after purchase. If cheeses are stored in the refrigerator, they should be left for an hour at room temperature before serving for the best flavor. Set out only as much as will be eaten, rather than allow cheese to remain at room temperature unnecessarily. Fresh cheeses such as *mozzarella* should be eaten right away.

To keep cheeses, wrap them in slightly dampened paper wrapped in a damp towel, or in waxed paper or aluminum foil, and store in the refrigerator. Plastic wrap does not allow cheese to breathe. Fresh *mozzarella*, however, suffers from refrigeration, as does *gorgonzola*. If they must be kept past the day of purchase, wrap them in foil and store in a cool place. *Mozzarella* and *mascarpone* can be frozen to store them for longer periods. Aged cheeses such as *parmigiano*, *pecorino* and *caciotta* continue to age and acquire flavor under refrigeration. Grate hard cheeses just before you are ready to use them, as their flavor diminishes quickly upon grating.

Cheeses are usually offered after the meal with fruits, not before. Certain cheeses,—*parmigiano-reggiano, gorgonzola in barchette* (little pastry "boats"), dripping-fresh *mozzarella*, and other fresh cheeses in particular—are offered as *antipasti,* however. Fresh cheeses are typically drizzled with flavorful extra-virgin olive oil and sprinkled with freshly ground black pepper.

COLD CUTS, in Italian, *salumi.* As with cheeses and numerous other Italian food products, the making of various *salumi* reflects local customs and traditions, with the result that countless variations exist from region to region. *Salumi* are sometimes produced at home, but even when they are manufactured in quantity for commercial consumption, they are made with a great deal of skill and concern for quality.

❋ **BRESAOLA,** a product of Valtellina in the region of Lombardy, is salted and air-dried fillet of beef. *Bresaola* has an aggressive flavor in comparision to *prosciutto.* It should be served as an *antipasto* with nothing more than a little extra-virgin olive oil drizzled over it, a splash of freshly squeezed lemon juice, and a veil of freshly milled black pepper. Marcella Hazan suggests Swiss Grison as an acceptable substitute, as imported Italian *bresaola* is unavailable in America. Both *bresaola* and Grison should be eaten soon after they are sliced–preferably within six hours, but certainly within twenty-four–as once cut they dry out and lose flavor quickly.

❋ **CAPOCOLLO,** a cooked shoulder ham fairly well-known in America, is prepared differently throughout the Italian regions, although perhaps the most renowned versions come from Apulia and Calabria. It is often flavored with salt, pepper, sugar, nutmeg, and white wine.

❋ **CULATELLO** is a ham made from the buttock of the pig immediately after butchering. It is not as refined as prosciutto crudo, nor cured in the same way. It is a moist ham, flavored with white wine or other liquor and sometimes spices such as juniper and pepper.

❋ **MORTADELLA** resembles a very large American baloney with little white circles of fat throughout. This is a specialty of Bologna, from whence came the name of the American meat that otherwise bears little resemblance to the original. *Mortadella* is made from very finely minced high-quality pork (one of the essential differences from American baloney, which is made from pork scraps). Whole peppercorns and other spices are added before the mixture is formed into a huge sausage and cooked. *Mortadella* of fine quality is buttery tender, subtle but immensely flavorful. We can buy good *mortadella* here, and it is not difficult to find.

❋ **PANCETTA** has no American equivalent. It is an unsmoked Italian bacon (*pancia* is Italian for belly, in this case, pig's belly), cured with salt and mild spices, usually pepper and a hint of cloves. In Italy, it is produced in a slab or a roll, but here only the rolled variety is available. Many specialty-food shops carry it. Avoid *pancetta* that is mostly fat; look for a good deal of meat running through it. American bacon can be substituted, but remember that it will add a strong smoky taste to your dish. To minimize bacon's smoky taste, blanch it for one minute before using it.

❋ **PROSCIUTTO** is a general term for ham (*prosciugare* means "to dry"), including *prosciutto cotto,* or "cooked ham" much like conventional boiled ham in America, and *prosciutto crudo,* the remarkable uncooked, air-dried, salt-cured ham of Italy. The most famous *prosciutti crudi* are produced in Langhirano, in the province of Parma, which lies in the region of Emilia-Romagna, and in San Daniele, in the region of Friuli. In Parma, the pigs are fed on the whey from the *parmigiano-reggiano* cheese that is a specialty of Emilia.

There are many different types of *prosciutti,* varying from region to region. The United States Food and Drug Administration banned the import of *prosciutto* and other pork products from Italy for twenty-two years because of an outbreak of African swine fever among some livestock. *Prosciutto*-producing pigs were never affected, but manufacturers were nonetheless forbidden to export all Italian-made *salumi* to the United States until 1989. *Prosciutto* produced in Switzerland, the United States, and Canada is fashioned after the Parma original, but is generally saltier and tougher; in addition, these products are also sometimes cooked rather than air-dried and salt-cured.

The *prosciutto crudo* produced today in Italy is a result of two thousand years of evolution in Parma ham making. Its ancestors, made from wild boars that roamed the Parma forests, were highly salted. Renaissance recipes suggest the addition of vinegar, wine, and such flavorings as coriander, fennel, and cloves. Today's *prosciutto* is made of only four ingredients: hand-selected legs of the most pampered pigs in the world, salt, air, and skill.

Today's premier *prosciutto* makers pride themselves on being able to produce the hams with as little salt as possible: the greater the maker, the less salt used. No sugar or nitrates are added, even though a small percentage of preservatives is allowed by law. *Conoscenti* describe the best *prosciutto crudo* with much the same passion and precision that oenophiles talk about wines: each slice should have a creamy rim of fat around it, and the fragrance of the meat should conjure hay, vineyards, and earth–aromas that come from the breezes that blow through the windows of the buildings in which *prosciutti* are hung to dry. Its color should be rosy, never sallow. The natural sweetness of pork should come through, but the taste should be complex. Salt is just a backdrop and should never be prominent. The meat and the fat that surrounds it should be so tender as almost to melt in the mouth. The tasty rim of fat surrounding a slice of *prosciutto* is an integral part of the *prosciutto* experience. The flesh should be supple, not at all resistant to the bite.

❋ **SALAME** is made in countless varieties, both *cotti* ("cooked") and *crudi* ("raw," or salted and air-dried), throughout the Italian regions. Italians are as adamant about the superiority of their respective *salami* as they are about other aspects of their localized cuisine. Among the most famous is Tuscan *finocchiona*, a large, soft salame flavored with fennel seeds. Another is *soppressata*, a flavorful, meaty *salame* from southern Italy whose uses go beyond the *affettato* (sliced cured meat) platter. It is added to bean, rice, and vegetable salads; stuffings; sauces; and fillings for *calzone*, fritters, and the like. *Coppa*, pork spiced with pepper, nutmeg, and orange peel, is an interesting *salame* from the Marches region; it is boiled rather than air-cured. Abruzzi is well-known for a similar pork *salame* that is flavored with *peperoncino* (hot red pepper), fennel, and orange peel. Only a small number of these delicious *salami* are exported, and those that are are most often produced industrially. Nevertheless, many of them are very good.

MUSHROOMS, in Italian, *funghi*. Cultivated mushrooms are not interchangeable with either fresh or dried wild mushrooms. Of all the wild mushrooms, *porcini*, *Boletus edulus* in Latin and known as *cèpes* in France, are the most prized in Italian cooking. There are three varieties of *Boletus*, all called *porcini*. *Boletus pinicola* (also known as *pinaroli*) grow around pine and Douglas fir. While they are the most beautiful, they do not have as much flavor as *Boletus edulus*. A more flavorful variety is *Boletus arias*, which grows in mixed wooded areas in Italy and the lower Southwest of the United States. Immensely flavorful with a rich, woodsy aroma that is positively intoxicating, *Boletus edulus* is the most sought-after and tastiest variety. The mushrooms grow under broad-leafed trees such as chestnut, oak, poplar, and hazelnut, and sometimes reach enormous size. (These wild *porcini* grow so large in Italy that they are eaten as a main course, sautéed in olive oil with garlic and fresh parsley, each cap the size of a steak, or as *cappelle di porcini al forno*, roasted whole in the oven.)

Fresh *porcini* are among the most perishable wild mushrooms and lose a great deal of flavor after just four days. Restaurants sometimes buy flash-frozen *porcini*, which can have better flavor than fresh *porcini* that have been kept too long at the market. (They should not, however, be defrosted before cooking because their structure will break down and they will become soggy. Instead, blanch them immediately after removing them from the freezer, then cook them.)

Dried *funghi porcini* are the most practical alternative to the hard-to-find fresh *porcini*. They retain much of their wonderful flavor (drying, in fact, concentrates it). Buy only the fleshy, predominantly light-colored part of the mushroom, not the dark, gnarled pieces, which are not as good. Dried *porcini* are very expensive, but it only takes a small amount to impart a powerful flavor. Many other types of dried wild mushrooms are available in America, including *chanterelles,* morels, and French *cèpes.*

To use dried mushroooms, soak them in warm water for thirty minutes. Remove them from the water, reserving the water, rinse in clear water only if they are still sandy, and then squeeze dry. Cut them in whatever way the recipe indicates. Strain the soaking water through a paper towel to remove any grit, and save it for use in sauces or stock.

Other varieties of fresh wild mushrooms–*chanterelles,* oyster mushrooms, *shiitake,* hedgehog mushrooms–are becoming more common in large city markets and specialty grocers. When cooking wild mushrooms, I like to combine *shiitake,* which have a firm texture, with *chanterelles,* morels, and oyster mushrooms, which are tasty and tender, for an interesting contrast of flavors and textures.

Fresh cultivated mushrooms have their place in Italian cooking, although the white varieties readily available here are very bland. They cannot stand on their own in a mushroom sauce, and should be combined with dried *porcini* if used for this purpose.

Fresh mushrooms lose their texture if they are washed, so it is best to dust them with a dry cotton towel or a mushroom brush. If they are sandy and gritty, wash them quickly in cold water (do not soak them) and dry immediately and thoroughly.

OLIVES, in Italian, *olive.* Black, green, brown, and purple olives all come from the same fruit, the green being the youngest and the black, the oldest. To the Italians, the French, and the peoples of the Middle East, olives can constitute an entire meal. Certainly, they are essential to the *antipasto* table, where they are treated in a variety of ways: added to salads and other dishes or stuffed with a mixture of *prosciutto,* minced veal, and savory bread filling and deep-fried.

The virtually tasteless pitted, canned olives and the highly salted stuffed cocktail-variety olives that are ubiquitous in America should not be substituted for properly cured olives from the Mediterranean region. There are many good imported Italian, French, Greek, and Spanish olives available, packed in brine or preserved in olive oil. A nice thing to do is to marinate these olives with herbs. For Umbrian-style olives, cover good imported black olives with olive oil, strips of orange peel, and bay leaves. For a variation with imported green olives, use fresh branches of rosemary in place of the bay leaves. Green olives are also superb in a marinade of olive oil, *peperoncini* (hot red peppers), and lots of bruised garlic cloves. Be sure to cover the olives with at least an inch of olive oil, and they will last in the marinade forever. If they are well submerged in oil, there is no need to refrigerate them.

OLIVE OIL, in Italian, *olio di oliva.* The olive tree is imbued with symbolic meaning in the imaginations and mythologies of Mediterranean cultures. Its existence merges with the very origins of civilization itself in the Mediterranean basin. The first olive seed is said to have germinated in the Earthly Paradise, and sprouted from the grave of Adam. In the Book of Genesis, Noah releases a dove that returns with an olive twig in its beak, a symbol of the end of the flood and of God's wrath. Jacob, when he sees a ladder reaching toward heaven, anoints the rock upon which he had lain with olive oil, transforming it into a sacred stone. Before his death, Jesus goes into an olive grove to pray, and weeps.

Olive oil is still used today in Christian holy rites. The symbolic meaning ascribed to the oil clearly merges with the political and economic importance of the fruits and the oil. Both the Etruscans and the ancient Romans based their cooking on olive oil and the practice continues to this day in Italy. Certainly, its rich, aromatic flavor is critical in the preparation of many *antipasti*.

Where only industrial quality, chemically treated, refined olive oils were once found in America, now many olive oils are available. Olive oil is graded according to the percentage of oleic acid it contains. The lower the level of acidity, the better the flavor of the oil. Extra-virgin olive oil contains less than 1 percent acidity. Olive oil labeled virgin has an acid content of up to 1.5 percent. So-called pure olive oils contain up to 3 percent acidity. The best quality is extra-virgin olive oil, what the Italians call either *spremuto a freddo* (cold pressed) or *prima spremitura* (first pressed). This refers to the oil released from the first pressing of young olives that have just started to turn green. (If the olives are too mature, their acidity level is too high.) It is costly because it is difficult, labor-intensive (premium extra-virgin olive oil is a completely handmade product, from the picking of the olives to the pressing), and time-consuming to produce, and only a small quantity of this grade can be extracted from a batch of olives.

Because the olives should not be bruised, they must be taken directly from the tree, not collected from the ground. They should be pressed the same day, and no later than the second day after harvesting. The olives are immediately washed, then crushed between large stone wheels into a paste. The oil is extracted from the paste, then passed through filters. A centrifuge separates the oil from the water in the fruit, after which the oil may be filtered. The best-quality extra-virgin olive oil is extracted without the use of chemicals. The paste that remains is then treated chemically in order to distill it, and results in lesser-quality olive oil. Anything less than extra-virgin olive oil has been treated chemically.

By law, Italian extra-virgin olive oil cannot exceed 1 percent acidity, and must be produced by pressing the olives, not by chemical extraction. American olive oils can be called extra-vir-

gin without having to adhere to these strict guidelines for classification. Sadly, there is much fraud in the production of extra-virgin olive oil produced outside of Italy, and much of what is sold for the real thing is relatively tasteless. The indicators of true extra-virgin olive oil are found in its flavor, aroma, and color; also, in its price. Because it is labor-intensive to produce and rare, it is very costly.

Olive oils vary in taste according to the type of olive (120 different varieties are used), climatic variations, and soil, as well as processing. While there can be no hard and fast rules because there are so many climatic variations within regions, there are general characteristics that hold true. Southern Italian oils are considered "riper" and thicker; Ligurian oils are golden and delicately flavored; northern Italian oils are peppery and pungent; oils from Tuscany, Umbria, and central Italy are very fruity. Experts say that oils from warmer climates don't last long–perhaps not even as long as a year–while oils from cooler climates might last up to three years.

Olive oil is at its best when it is very young. The taste and aroma of just-pressed oil is exquisite. If you are in Italy during olive-pressing time in December, you might find your way to a *fattoria* where it is done. It is well worth the effort to get a taste of the first day's pressed oil, dribbled onto a toasted slab of country bread. I prefer the stronger flavor and aroma of the cloudy, fruity, unfiltered first-pressed oil for most types of cooking, although unfiltered oil turns rancid more quickly than filtered oil. Both are a rich green-gold that is unmistakable when compared to the pale gold of the lesser grades that come from subsequent pressings. Although heating extra-virgin olive oil causes it to lose some of its flavor and aroma, it is superior used in everything from dressings to sautéing and baking. The Italians use it extravagantly, even for deep-frying (*calamari* fried in extra-virgin olive oil have no equal). I have indicated throughout this book where it is essential to use extra-virgin olive oil. In other recipes, it should be used if it is affordable; otherwise substitute virgin olive oil. For frying, use so-called pure olive oil.

It is very important for olive oil to be fresh, because as it ages, its fruity flavor turns rancid. Light and heat will cause it to deteriorate quickly. Many olive oils on the market are stale before they are ever purchased. Buy in small quantities from a store where merchandise moves quickly (keep in mind that the new vintage arrives every winter, usually around January), and use it frequently. The best grade extra-virgin olive oils are often numbered and vintage-dated, which enables buyers to be assured of both the freshness and purity of premium extra-virgin oils. The best way to keep olive oil is to store it capped in a cool place. Do not refrigerate it, and do not store it near a direct source of heat. Nor should you ever top it with fresh oil from a new bottle. Using it often is the best way to keep it fresh.

One of the best things about olive oil is that it is healthful as well as delicious. Recent studies show that because of its properties as a "monounsaturate," it will lower excessive levels of cholesterol in the blood.

Olive oil is excellent for cooking not only because of its flavor, but also because it has the highest smoking point of any oil. But the best way to experience the full, clear taste of extra-virgin olive oil is to use it cold, as is done in so many *antipasto* dishes.

PINE NUTS, in Italian, *pinoli* or *pignoli.* These are the nuts or kernels of the cones of stone pines, which are found along stretches of the Italian coastline. They are used extensively in the Italian kitchen, in Sicilian *caponata* (sweet-and-sour eggplant), rice salads, stuffings, ground in Ligurian potato croquettes (known as *cuculli di patate*), in baked goods and confections. They turn rancid quickly, so it is best to refrigerate or freeze them. Because their texture is softer than that of most nuts, they should be very lightly toasted before using. And

because they are so small and oily, they burn in an instant, so stand over them when toasting!

TOMATOES, in Italian, *pomodori.* The tomatoes used in Italian cooking are the sweet, soft, fleshy "plum" variety, which are difficult to grow in colder climates. Cherry tomatoes can be substituted, for they are sweet, although they take some patience to peel and seed. Good vine-ripened tomatoes have no equal, and it is these sweet tomatoes that are intended in recipes calling for fresh tomatoes. Refrigerating tomatoes will certainly kill much of their flavor. Do not buy tomatoes that have been refrigerated, and leave them at room temperature until you are ready to use them. Imported and some domestic canned plum tomatoes can be excellent, and certainly can be substituted in sauces or dishes where the tomatoes are cooked.

SUN-DRIED TOMATOES, in Italian, *pomodori secchi.* Despite their popularity in America, these are little known in most of Italy except for the deep south (Sardinia in particular), where they are harvested at the end of the summer and dried in the sun for winter use. They are then packed in salt and sometimes formed into large loaves. Pieces are sliced off when needed for cooking, or just to spread on bread. They can be made into a pesto with olive oil and garlic for pasta (see my book, *Pasta Classica: The Art of Italian Pasta Cooking*), or blanched, peeled, chopped, and added to tomato, meat, or vegetable-based sauces for body and a piquant flavor. In Sardinia, they are added to stews, stuffings, winter *cassola* (fish soup), and fillings for *impanadas* (meat or meat-and-vegetable pies). They are never, as is the fashion in America, presented whole on a dish, being quite leathery and unappetizingly strong flavored in their dried state. As a component in a dish with other ingredients, however, they add marvelous flavor. They can be used with cheese, olives, and other ingredients in fillings for savory breads, *focaccie,* and so on.

To reconstitute sun-dried tomatoes that are not preserved in oil, cover them with boiling water and let them stand for fifteen minutes. Drain and pat dry thoroughly. Lay them out on a baking sheet and place in an oven preheated to 250 degrees F for ten minutes. Transfer to a jar and add olive oil to cover and a few peppercorns and peeled garlic cloves. Preserved this way, dried tomatoes will keep for a long time in the refrigerator. If at least an inch of olive oil covers the tomatoes, they can be held without refrigeration.

TUNA, in Italian, *tonno sott'olio.* The best tuna to use in *antipasti,* Italian salads, and sauces is the widely available imported pink-fleshed, moist Italian tuna packed in olive oil. It is from the belly of the fish, the most tender and flavorful part. Americans are accustomed to eating the white meat of the tuna, which is much drier (especially if it is packed in spring water instead of oil). This tasty Italian tuna appears in many guises on the *antipasto* table: combined with boiled eggs, potatoes, cooked vegetables, and homemade mayonnaise in lenten salads; with purèed potatoes in *polpettone* ("meatloaf" of sorts) in cooked and uncooked versions; in a sausage that is served with a sauce of extra-virgin olive oil, capers, pickles, and parsley; in stuffing for eggs; in a buttery spread for *crostini;* tossed with *cannellini* beans, parsley, sliced sweet onion, and extra-virgin olive oil. In the classic *vitello tonnato* (page 63), it is ground and mixed with homemade mayonnaise for a sauce to blanket cold poached veal.

VINEGAR, in Italian, *aceto.* Vinegar is made from many foods, including beer, fruit, grain, rice, and wine. The most complex and delicate vinegars are made from red or white wine. According to Italian law, vinegar must be made from the fermentation of wine. Red wine vinegars are aged, like great wines, in wooden casks for six months or longer,

and then allowed to rest in stainless-steel vessels. White wine vinegars are aged for a period of one year before they are transferred to stainless-steel containers to age further. But not all wine vinegars are alike. Poor-quality wines and lack of skill or care in the vinegar-making process result in inferior vinegars. Italian vinegars of quality, which should have 7 percent acidity, are regulated by government standards to ensure their character. The percentage of acidity marked on the label–from 5 to 7 percent–indicates the tartness of the vinegar; the higher the percentage, the tarter the vinegar.

❀ **BALSAMIC VINEGAR** (literally, "healthful" vinegar) is in a category of its own. This extraordinary vinegar was all but unheard of in America until Italian food authority and cookbook author Marcella Hazan introduced it in her writings. Made in Modena, in the region of Emilia-Romagna, from the boiled-down must of the sweet, white *Trebbiano* grape, the vinegar is aged in casks of five or six different woods, including juniper, chestnut, mulberry, cherry, oak, and ash, of gradually diminishing size. Each of the woods imparts its own particular color and aroma, which combined, influence the deep, mellow, and complex flavor and aroma of the vinegar. By law, balsamic vinegar must be aged for at least ten years, although it can be aged for decades. The longer it ages, the more dense the vinegar, and the more subtle and "round" the flavor. The best balsamic vinegar is aged for at least twenty years.

Traditionally, balsamic vinegar was only used on meats. Until recent years, leafy salads were not eaten in Italy, but now the vinegar is used alone in salads. No oil is necessary because of the dense, mellow flavor of the vinegar. Balsamic vinegar is used in cooking, but only at the last minute, as a flavoring for grilled meats, or it is combined with other ingredients in raw sauces. It adds wonderful flavor to vegetable *antipasti,* raw or cooked, or to *spiedini* (skewered meats). ❀❀❀

CHAPTER 2

VEGETABLES & SALADS

* * *

Antipasti di verdura

VEGETABLES

are not afterthoughts on the Italian table. In the south of Italy, where historically meat has been scarce, vegetables, along with pasta, have been the focus of daily meals. Throughout the region, they are cooked in *pasticci* ("casseroles"), baked into pies, braised, stuffed, grilled, roasted, fried, sautéed, boiled, stewed, made into pasta sauces and stuffings, and eaten raw. Put simply, vegetables are prepared in every way imaginable. In the north, even with its greater abundance of meat, they always have been treated with great creativity. Indeed, no matter where one travels in Italy, every local market teems with a dazzling array of *verdura*. Even in Sardinia, where the summer climate is torrid and one would think that many vegetables could not withstand the intense dry heat and sandy soil, the markets offer an extraordinary selection. ❋ The greatest difference between such local produce and the mass-produced vegetables grown for American markets is flavor. Even though American supermarket artichokes can *look* enticing, giant and richly green with purple blushes, they do not *taste* the way artichokes can taste. Why are they grown so large? The best artichokes are tiny, just as the best zucchini are quite small, not overgrown, tough, and full of seeds. Likewise, tomatoes in America are rarely the sweet, luscious fruits they should be. Everything from cabbages to potatoes, in their ideal state, are more flavorful than one might ever imagine who has never had a garden, or bought fresh produce ripened under the Mediterranean sun. ❋ To achieve the greatest success in Italian cooking, purchase vegetables at their freshest. The skins of peppers, eggplants, squashes, and other vegetables should be firm and taut, never wrinkled. Most vegetables are crisp when they are fresh, never limp. There should be no signs of deterioration: mold, softness at the touch, dark spots on the skin. Frozen vegetables, with the exception of peas, are never a substitute. And canned vegetables, with the exception of canned plum tomatoes, are simply unthinkable in authentic Italian cooking. Try to approximate the experience of shopping in an Italian market by seeking out the best purveyors, and then picking and choosing the vegetables carefully. ❁ Every Italian family has its own ways with vegetables. In my house, inspired as it was by my mother's girlhood in Sardinia, artichokes (the quintessential Sardinian vegetable) basked in a delicious hot bath redolent with the scents of olive oil, garlic, and thyme. In my aunt's house, on the other hand, artichokes were baked Sardinian style with *prosciutto,* fresh *pecorino,* and wine for a magnificent *antipasto* or side dish. (In traditional Sardinian cooking, *antipasti* were not served, but this has changed since World War II, particularly in the cities.) In fact, throughout Italy cooking styles vary so much from region to region, town to town, and family to family, that one can be assured there will never be an end to the number of different ways in which vegetables are prepared. ❁ There are traditionally two courses on the Italian table where vegetables predominate. One is the *contorno,* or the side dish that is brought along with or after the main course. And the other is the *antipasto* course. But it is on the *antipasto* table that vegetables are treated most imaginatively, for here dishes are designed to provoke the appetite in anticipation of what will follow. ❁ Although this is by far the largest chapter in the book, there could have been many more vegetable recipes. In the end I chose my favorites and those that I expect are least familiar, as well as some classic recipes I have interpreted in my own way. ❁ ❁ ❁

ANTIPASTO DI MAGRO

FAST-DAY SALAD WITH TUNA, POTATOES, EGGS, AND GREEN BEANS

FOR 4 PEOPLE

❋

CANNED ITALIAN TUNA IS A MARVELOUS PRODUCT, WITH A MYRIAD OF USES IN THE ITALIAN KITCHEN. IT IS A DELIGHT IN SALADS, PARTICULARLY IN THIS ONE, PERHAPS MY FAVORITE. THERE ARE MANY VARIATIONS OF *antipasto di magro*, SO-CALLED BECAUSE THERE IS NO MEAT IN IT. *Magro* MEANS "LEAN," A TERM OFTEN ASSIGNED TO DISHES SERVED ON CHRISTIAN FAST DAYS WHEN MEAT EATING IS TRADITIONALLY FORBIDDEN. WHILE THE SALAD CAN BE SERVED WITH EXTRA-VIRGIN OLIVE OIL AND GOOD RED WINE VINEGAR, THE BEST DRESSING IS A LEMONY HOMEMADE MAYONNAISE. IT IS BEST TO USE IMPORTED ITALIAN TUNA PACKED IN OLIVE OIL, WHICH IS SWEETER AND MORE TENDER THAN THE AMERICAN BRANDS THAT PACK THE DRIER WHITE ALBACORE TUNA.

❋ *½ pound waxy boiling potatoes (about 5 small)*

❋ *3 eggs*

❋ *1 teaspoon salt*

❋ *½ pound green beans, trimmed*

❋ *1 can (6-½ ounces) imported Italian light tuna in olive oil, drained and flaked*

❋ *2 tablespoons thinly slivered red onion (about 1 inch long)*

❋ *½ recipe Light Lemon Mayonnaise (page 127)*

❋ *1 tablespoon drained small capers*

❶ PUT THE UNPEELED POTATOES in a pot with enough cold water to cover and bring to a boil over high heat. Immediately reduce the heat to medium and cook until tender when pierced with a cake tester or sharp knife, about 20 minutes. Drain and, when cool enough to handle, peel the potatoes and cut them crosswise into ¼-inch-thick slices.

❷ MEANWHILE, place the eggs in a saucepan with cold water to cover and bring to a boil. Cook them for a total of 15 minutes from the time they are placed on the stove. Drain and shell them while they are still warm so that they will slip out of their shells easily, then allow to cool before cutting crosswise into ¼-inch-thick slices.

❸ AT THE SAME TIME, fill another saucepan with water and bring to a boil. Add the salt first, then the green beans, and boil, uncovered, until tender, about 7 minutes. (The salt helps the beans to retain their color.) Drain and set aside. The beans will cool somewhat, but it is best if they are still warm when combined with the other ingredients so they are receptive to the dressing and other flavors.

❹ IN A SALAD BOWL, preferably of clear glass, layer first the potatoes, then the tuna, onion, green beans, and eggs, spooning a little mayonnaise atop each layer before arranging the next one. Spoon more mayonnaise on top and scatter on the capers. Serve within 2 hours of preparing.

MELANZANE FRITTE

DEEP-FRIED EGGPLANT

FOR 6 PEOPLE

THIS IS A TYPICAL ITALIAN WAY OF FRYING VEGETABLES, FISH, MEAT CUTLETS, AND OTHER FOODS. DREDGING THE FOOD IN FLOUR BEFORE COATING IT WITH BEATEN EGG AND THEN CRUMBS MAKES IT DELIGHTFULLY CRUNCHY. EGGPLANT IS PARTICULARLY DELICIOUS COOKED IN THIS STYLE. ❋ FOR THE BEST RESULTS WITH EGGPLANT, SELECT ONLY THE FRESHEST ONES, AND AVOID EXCESSIVELY LARGE FRUITS, AS THEY CONTAIN TOO MANY SEEDS. PASS OVER THOSE THAT HAVE WRINKLED SKIN, AN INDICATION OF AGE, OR THOSE WITH BRUISES. TO DETERMINE MATURITY, PRESS THE SKIN WITH YOUR FINGERTIP. IF IT IS PERFECTLY HARD, IT IS PROBABLY NOT RIPE. IT SHOULD BE RESILIENT TO THE TOUCH, BUT NOT SOFT ENOUGH TO FORM AN INDENTATION. THE WHITE AND PINK EGGPLANT VARIETIES HAVE FEWER BITTER SEEDS THAN THE PURPLE ONES, BUT THEY ARE LESS FLAVORFUL. ❋ ZUCCHINI ARE ALSO DELICIOUS DEEP-FRIED. IF THEY ARE FRESH AND SMALL, THERE IS NO NEED TO SALT THEM AS YOU WOULD EGGPLANT.

❋ *1 large eggplant (1-¼ to 1-½ pounds)*
❋ *salt*
❋ *2 extra-large eggs*
❋ *large pinch of freshly grated nutmeg (about ⅛ teaspoon)*
❋ *½ cup all-purpose flour or unbleached white flour*
❋ *1 cup fine dried bread crumbs*
❋ *olive oil for deep-frying*

❶ CUT OFF THE STEM and the navel of the eggplant, but do not peel. Cut lengthwise into ½-inch-thick slices. Lightly sprinkle both sides of each slice with salt. Stand the slices upright lengthwise in a colander, so that the liquid released will escape through the colander bottom. Let stand for 30 minutes.

❷ GENTLY WIPE OFF THE SWEAT from the eggplant slices with a cloth towel. Cut into lengthwise strips approximately 3 inches long and 1 inch wide. Beat the eggs with the nutmeg in a wide, shallow bowl. To one side of the bowl, place the flour on a piece of waxed paper; to the opposite side, place the bread crumbs on a second sheet of waxed paper.

❸ POUR ENOUGH OLIVE OIL into a large, deep skillet to reach 1 inch up the sides of the pan. Place over medium-high heat until it is hot enough (375 degrees F) to make the eggplant sizzle instantly. Dip the eggplant strips into the flour, then into the egg, and finally into the bread crumbs, coating them thoroughly and evenly each time. Slip them into the hot oil and fry on both sides until golden and crisp, about 6 minutes in all. Do not crowd the pan; give each strip plenty of room in which to cook. The eggplant will not absorb too much oil as long as the oil is very hot. Remove with a slotted spoon and drain on paper towels or brown paper. Keep the eggplant in a warm oven while you fry the remaining strips. Sprinkle with salt, if desired. Serve immediately, as they should be eaten quite hot.

ZUCCHINE MARINATE

MARINATED ZUCCHINI

FOR 4 TO 6 PEOPLE

✸

MARINATING IN THIS MANNER IS A VENERABLE METHOD FOR PRESERVING A VARIETY OF COOKED VEGETABLES. ITALIANS SOMETIMES REFER TO THE DISH AS *ascapece,* POSSIBLY FROM THE SPANISH *escabeche.* WHILE THE CLASSIC METHOD IS TO DEEP-FRY THE THINLY SLICED VEGETABLES IN OLIVE OIL AND THEN LAYER THEM IN A DISH, STREWING GOOD-QUALITY WINE VINEGAR, CHOPPED GARLIC, AND PARSLEY OR MINT IN BETWEEN, I PREFER TO RUB THE SLICED ZUCCHINI WITH EXTRA-VIRGIN OLIVE OIL AND THEN ROAST THEM IN AN OVEN, OR GRILL THEM OVER CHARCOAL, BEFORE MARINATING. SERVE THIS DISH AS AN *antipasto* OR AS A SIDE DISH WITH GRILLED OR ROASTED MEATS.

✳ *2 pounds young, firm zucchini (preferably no more than 6 ounces each)*
✳ *extra-virgin olive oil as needed*
✳ *5 large cloves garlic, sliced*
✳ *¼ cup chopped fresh basil, mint, or Italian parsley*
✳ *¼ cup red wine vinegar*
✳ *salt and freshly milled black pepper*

❶ PREHEAT AN OVEN to 500 degrees F. Cut off the stems and navels from the zucchini and cut lengthwise into ⅛-inch-thick slices. Generously brush 2 baking sheets with olive oil. Place the zucchini slices on the sheets and brush the tops with more olive oil. Bake on the middle rack of the preheated oven until tender and beginning to brown, 15 to 20 minutes, turning them once halfway through the cooking, and brushing the second side with more olive oil. To grill the zucchini slices, see method for Grilled Vegetables (page 31).

❷ Select a serving dish in which you will be able to put at least 3 layers of the cooked zucchini slices. Arrange some of the zucchini slices in a single layer. Drizzle generously with olive oil. Strew over some of the garlic slices and the basil, mint, or parsley, and sprinkle with some of the vinegar and with salt and pepper to taste. Continue to layer the zucchini slices and other ingredients in this same manner until the zucchini and garlic have all been used. Sprinkle the top layer with olive oil and sprinkle with salt, pepper, and vinegar. Cover and chill overnight.

❸ Bring to room temperature the following day before serving. The zucchini will keep well, refrigerated, for several days, but the flavor sharpens.

NOTE: A variation is to stuff the marinated zucchini slices with sharp-flavored black olives, cubes of fresh *mozzarella,* or cold, freshly cooked shrimp. To prepare, roll up each marinated zucchini slice from a narrow end and slip an olive, cube of fresh *mozzarella,* or cooked shrimp in the middle. Thread a toothpick at an angle through each little bundle to keep it intact. Serve at room temperature.

INVOLTINI DI ZUCCHINE

ZUCCHINI ROLLS STUFFED WITH RICOTTA

FOR 6 PEOPLE

HERE IS A FACSIMILE OF A DISH I HAD AT THE HOME OF KAREN FORHALTZ AND MICHAEL MIELE, THE CHEF-OWNERS OF A NICE LITTLE NEW YORK EATERY CALLED AMSTERDAM'S. THE TWO RESTAURATEURS ARE INVETERATE TRAVELERS TO ITALY, AND THEIR TABLE—HOME AND RESTAURANT—IS ALWAYS FULL OF GOOD ITALIAN THINGS TO EAT. THERE ARE THREE STAGES TO THIS RECIPE: MAKING THE SAUCE, PREBAKING THE SLICED ZUCCHINI, AND MAKING THE FILLING AND STUFFING THE ZUCCHINI WITH IT. I ALWAYS LIKE TO MAKE THE TOMATO SAUCE, SIMPLE AS IT IS, IN ADVANCE, SO THAT ONLY TWO STEPS ARE NECESSARY WHEN IT IS TIME TO ASSEMBLE THE DISH.

* 1 recipe Sieved Tomato Sauce with Basil (page 134)
* 4 young, firm zucchini (6 to 8 ounces each)
* extra-virgin olive oil for brushing on baking sheets and zucchini

For the filling:
* ¾ pound (1 ½ cups) ricotta, placed in a sieve for 1 to 2 hours to drain excess liquid
* ¼ cup freshly grated parmigiano
* ⅛ teaspoon freshly grated nutmeg
* 1 egg yolk
* salt and freshly milled black pepper

❶ FIRST MAKE THE SAUCE. Meanwhile, preheat an oven to 375 degrees F.

❷ CUT OFF THE STEMS and navels from the zucchini and cut lengthwise into 1/8-inch-thick slices. Lightly brush 2 baking sheets with olive oil. Place the zucchini slices on the sheets and brush the tops lightly with more olive oil. Bake in the preheated oven until soft but not browned, 15 to 20 minutes. Remove from the oven and allow to cool.

❸ WHILE THE ZUCCHINI IS BAKING, smear the bottom of an 11-by-14-inch baking pan with some of the tomato sauce and set aside. Combine all the ingredients for the filling, including salt and pepper to taste, in a bowl. Using a wooden spoon, beat until smooth. Place a teaspoonful of filling at the wider end of each zucchini slice and roll up the slice. Stand the zucchini rolls in the baking dish on top of the smeared sauce. They should be placed like an upright wheel, and not laid flat

with the filling facing up. Spoon additional sauce over the tops of the *involtini*. (You may have more sauce than you need; reserve what is left for some other use.)

❹ COVER THE BAKING DISH loosely with aluminum foil, dull side out, and bake in the preheated oven until sizzling, about 30 minutes. Allow to settle for 10 minutes before serving. Serve hot or warm.

AHEAD-OF-TIME NOTE: The tomato sauce can be made up to 3 days in advance, covered, and refrigerated. The zucchini slices can be baked, stuffed, covered, and refrigerated a day in advance. Pour the sauce over the top just before baking the rolls.

CIALED'

MY GRANDMOTHER'S ITALIAN BREAD SALAD

FOR 4 PEOPLE

✳

HERE IS A DISH MY FATHER TOLD ME ABOUT, WHICH HIS MOTHER MADE WHEN THEIR LIFE AS IMMIGRANTS WAS STILL VERY HARD AND THERE WAS LITTLE ELSE TO EAT BESIDES STALE BREAD. THE DISH IS NOT UNLIKE THE POPULAR TUSCAN SALAD CALLED *panzanella*. DESPITE ITS MOST HUMBLE ORIGINS, THIS SALAD IS DELICIOUS. THE BREAD MUST BE COARSE PEASANT BREAD OR ANY STURDY ITALIAN-STYLE BREAD. (MIDDLE EASTERN PITA BREAD WILL DO NICELY, TOO, EVEN THOUGH IT IS NOT ITALIAN.) OTHER BREADS WILL NOT HOLD UP TO BEING DRESSED WITH OIL AND VINEGAR, OR COMBINED WITH TOMATOES, WHICH ARE FULL OF WATER. NOR MUST BREAD THAT HAS BEEN SWEETENED WITH SUGAR OR HONEY BE USED. MOST IMPORTANT OF ALL, HOWEVER, IS THAT GOOD-QUALITY EXTRA-VIRGIN OLIVE OIL IS INDISPENSABLE.

✳ *½ loaf (about 1 pound) 2- to 3-day-old coarse peasant bread or sturdy Italian-style bread, crusts removed*

✳ *6 tablespoons water, or more, depending upon the dryness of the bread*

✳ *½ cup extra-virgin olive oil*

✳ *3 tablespoons red wine vinegar*

✳ *2 large, vine-ripened tomatoes or 4 plum tomatoes, seeded and diced*

✳ *½ red onion, sliced paper-thin*

✳ *2 tablespoons torn fresh basil or mint leaves*

✳ *2 teaspoons whole fresh oregano leaves, or 1 teaspoon dried oregano*

✳ *1 tablespoon chopped fresh Italian parsley*

✳ *½ teaspoon salt, or to taste*

✳ *¼ teaspoon freshly milled black pepper, or to taste*

❶ SLICE THE BREAD and then tear or cut it into 1-inch pieces. You should have approximately 6 cups. Place in a shallow bowl and sprinkle evenly with the 6 tablespoons water. If the bread is very dry, you may need to add another 1 or 2 tablespoons water.

❷ IN A SEPARATE BOWL, stir together the olive oil, vinegar, tomatoes, onion, and half of the herbs. Let marinate for 10 minutes. Pour over the bread, add the remaining herbs, and toss well. Season with the salt and pepper and serve.

AHEAD-OF-TIME NOTE: This salad can be made 1 or 2 hours in advance as long as a sturdy bread is used.

INSALATA DI BARBABIETOLE CON DRAGONCELLO

BEET SALAD WITH ORANGE AND TARRAGON

FOR 2 OR 3 PEOPLE

❊

MY MOTHER ALWAYS MADE BEET SALADS WHEN I WAS GROWING UP. WHILE I HATED HOT BEETS, I LOVED THEM COLD IN SALADS LIKE THIS ONE. IF POSSIBLE, SELECT YOUNG, SMALL BEETS, WHICH ARE MORE TENDER THAN LARGE BEETS AND TAKE FAR LESS TIME TO COOK. THIS SAME DRESSING IS LOVELY WITH SHREDDED RAW CARROTS, BUT SUBSTITUTE MINT FOR THE TARRAGON. (FOR CARROT SALAD, USE ONLY THE DARKER PART OF THE CARROT; DISCARD THE PALER, LESS SWEET, TOUGH INNER CORE.)

* *6 to 8 small to medium-sized beets*

FOR THE DRESSING:
* *2 tablespoons extra-virgin olive oil*
* *3 tablespoons freshly squeezed orange juice, preferably from a blood orange*
* *2 tablespoons balsamic vinegar*
* *1 teaspoon freshly grated orange zest*
* *1 tablespoon finely snipped fresh tarragon, or 2 teaspoons dried tarragon*
* *salt and freshly milled black pepper*

❶ TRIM THE LEAVES OFF THE BEETS, but do not remove the tops or pierce the beets themselves, or their juice will bleed into the water and flavor and color will be lost. Fill a saucepan with enough water to cover the beets generously and bring to a rapid boil. Add the beets and reduce the heat so that the beets boil gently until tender, 20 to 30 minutes. When you can pierce them easily with a sharp knife, thin skewer, or, better yet, a cake tester, they are done. (Try to use something as thin as possible to prevent the beets from bleeding excessively when they are pierced.) They should be tender but not mushy.

❷ MEANWHILE, IN A SMALL BOWL, combine all the dressing ingredients, including salt and pepper to taste. Whisk to blend.

❸ WHEN THE BEETS ARE COOKED, drain them into cold water to cool so they can be handled. Drain again and cut off the tops and slip off the skins. Cut into 1/4-inch-thick slices and place in a salad bowl. Pour over the dressing, toss well, and serve. The beets can also be left to marinate at room temperature for several hours.

AHEAD-OF-TIME NOTE: This entire dish can be prepared a day in advance, covered, and refrigerated. Bring to room temperature before serving.

FUNGHI AL FORNO ALLA PARMIGIANA

BAKED WHOLE MUSHROOMS WITH PARMIGIANO

FOR 4 PEOPLE

❊

HERE IS AN ELEGANT AND VERSATILE DISH THAT CAN BE SERVED AS A STARTER, AS A VEGETABLE MAIN COURSE IN LARGER PORTIONS, OR AS A SIDE DISH WITH ROASTED MEAT, POULTRY, OR GAME. IT IS BEST MADE WITH WILD MUSHROOMS, BECAUSE THEY HAVE GREATER AND MORE COMPLEX FLAVORS AND MORE INTERESTING TEXTURES THAN THE CULTIVATED VARIETY.

❋ *1 pound fresh wild mushrooms such as
  chanterelle, porcini, hedgehog or oyster,
  or a mixture*
❋ *1 tablespoon water*

FOR THE TOPPING:
❋ *2 tablespoons freshly grated parmigiano*
❋ *1 tablespoon fine dried bread crumbs*
❋ *1 tablespoon chopped fresh Italian parsley*
❋ *¼ teaspoon chopped fresh thyme or marjoram,
  or a pinch of dried thyme or marjoram*
❋ *1 small clove garlic, finely chopped or
  passed through a garlic press*
❋ *salt and freshly milled black pepper*
❋ *extra-virgin olive oil for drizzling*

❶ PREHEAT AN OVEN to 350 degrees F. Remove any dirt from the mushrooms with a soft brush or dry cotton towel. Trim off the hard tips of the stems. If the mushrooms are extremely large, halve or quarter them lengthwise, depending upon their size.

❷ SELECT A BAKING PAN large enough to hold the mushrooms in a single layer and sprinkle the bottom with the water. Put the mushrooms in, stems up. In a small bowl, combine all the ingredients for the topping, including salt and pepper to taste, and mix thoroughly. Sprinkle the mixture evenly over the mushrooms. Drizzle generously with the olive oil. Bake, uncovered, in the preheated oven until the mushrooms are golden, about 15 minutes. Serve hot or warm.

PEPERONI ALLA NAPOLETANA

PLATTER OF ROASTED RED AND YELLOW PEPPERS WITH OLIVES, CAPERS, GARLIC, AND PARSLEY

FOR 4 PEOPLE

❊

THIS TRADITIONAL NEAPOLITAN RECIPE IS AS COLORFUL AS THE CITY AFTER WHICH IT IS NAMED. IT IS PROBABLY ONE OF MY FAVORITE WAYS OF PREPARING ROASTED PEPPERS—AS BEAUTIFUL AND TASTY AS IT IS SIMPLE.

❋ *2 large red bell peppers*
❋ *2 large yellow bell peppers*

FOR THE TOPPING:
❋ *2 teaspoons drained small capers or
  coarsely chopped large capers*
❋ *20 sharp-flavored black olives, pitted
  and sliced*
❋ *1 tablespoon chopped fresh Italian parsley*
❋ *½ small clove garlic, finely chopped or
  passed through a garlic press*
❋ *about 1 tablespoon extra-virgin olive oil
  for drizzling*

❶ ROAST THE PEPPERS as directed on page 28 and peel them. Cut each pepper into thirds lengthwise, following the natural contours of the pepper. Remove the stems, seeds, and ribs. Place the peppers on a serving platter, smooth side up, alternating the colors and forming a starlike arrangement.

❷ IN A SMALL BOWL, combine the ingredients for the topping and mix well. Strew the topping over the pepper sections in an attractive fashion, distributing it evenly. Drizzle with the olive oil. Serve at room temperature or chilled.

VARIATION: Add 2 anchovy fillets in olive oil, drained and cut up, to the topping.

AHEAD-OF-TIME NOTE: This dish can be prepared a day in advance, covered, and refrigerated.

PEPERONI ARROSTITI

ROASTED PEPPERS IN FOUR VARIATIONS

FOR 6 TO 8 PEOPLE

SMOKY ROASTED PEPPERS ARE AMONG THE MOST DELICIOUS OF VEGETABLES. I OFFER ONLY FOUR WAYS HERE THAT ROASTED PEPPERS CAN BE SERVED AS *antipasti*, BUT THE POSSIBILITIES ARE ENDLESS. RED, YELLOW, AND ORANGE BELL PEPPERS ARE SWEETER THAN THE GREEN ONES.

✳ *8 large red bell peppers, or a mixture of red, yellow, and orange bell peppers*

❶ ARRANGE THE PEPPERS on a grill rack above a charcoal fire, on wire racks positioned over the burners of a gas or electric stove, 2 to 3 inches under a preheated broiler, or in an oven preheated to 400 degrees F. Roast them until they are charred all over and tender inside, turning them frequently to ensure that they blacken evenly, about 30 minutes in the oven, but less time by the other methods. When the peppers are cool enough to handle, peel off the skins using your fingertips, cut the peppers in half, and remove and discard the stems, ribs, and seeds. (Do not do this under running water; it will wash away some of the delicious smoky flavor.)

ROASTED PEPPERS WITH ANCHOVIES: Cut the roasted, peeled, and seeded peppers into long strips about ¾ inch wide. Arrange on a plate, alternating the pepper strips with 16 anchovy fillets in olive oil, drained. Sprinkle with 1 small clove garlic, finely chopped, and drizzle lightly with extra-virgin olive oil. Serve at room temperature.

ROASTED PEPPERS WITH SWEET OR HOT ITALIAN SAUSAGES: Cut the roasted, peeled, and seeded peppers into long strips about 1 inch wide. Grill or broil 6 lean sweet or hot Italian sausages until they are evenly browned and cooked through. Cool slightly, then cut each one in half lengthwise. Arrange the sausages and roasted pepper strips on a platter, alternating them for an attractive presentation. Brush the pepper strips lightly with extra-virgin olive oil in which a bruised garlic clove has been infused. Serve hot or warm.

ROASTED PEPPERS WITH FRESH *mozzarella* AND BASIL: Divide the roasted, peeled, and seeded peppers into thirds following the natural contours of the peppers. Arrange them on a platter, smooth side up, alternating them with slices of fresh *mozzarella*. Drizzle lightly with extra-virgin olive oil and garnish with whole fresh basil leaves. Sprinkle with salt and dried red-pepper flakes to taste (remember, they are very spicy!). Serve at room temperature.

ROASTED PEPPERS WITH PARSLEY AND BLACK OLIVES: Cut the roasted, peeled, and seeded peppers into long strips about ¾ inch wide. Arrange them on a plate. Drizzle lightly with extra-virgin olive oil and strew with ¼ pound sharp-flavored black olives, pitted and sliced, and 2 tablespoons roughly chopped fresh Italian parsley. Serve at room temperature.

FINOCCHIO IN PINZIMONIO

FENNEL WITH PEPPERY OLIVE OIL DIP

FOR 2 OR 3 PEOPLE

❀

MANY VEGETABLES CAN BE EATEN RAW IN THIS RESOLUTELY UNPRETENTIOUS FASHION—DIPPED IN EXTRA-VIRGIN OLIVE OIL. THERE IS ONLY ONE CAVEAT: THE VEGETABLES MUST BE IMPECCABLY FRESH. FENNEL HEARTS; FRESHLY PICKED FAVA BEANS; STRIPS OF SWEET RED AND YELLOW PEPPERS; CAULIFLOWER FLORETS; CARROT, CELERY, CUCUMBER, AND ZUCCHINI STICKS; AND WEDGES OF VINE-RIPENED TOMATOES ARE ESPECIALLY GOOD. ❀ WHEN I WAS A LITTLE GIRL, MY MOTHER WOULD SOMETIMES HAVE RAW ARTICHOKES READY FOR US WHEN WE CAME HOME FROM SCHOOL. WE LOVED TO SIT AROUND THE KITCHEN TABLE AND RIP THE LEAVES OFF ONE BY ONE, THEN DIP THE BASE OF EACH INTO A LITTLE BOWL OF FRUITY OLIVE OIL SPRINKLED WITH SALT AND PEPPER. ONLY THE TENDER WHITE BASE OF THE LEAF WAS GOOD TO EAT. WE SCRAPED IT OFF BETWEEN OUR TEETH AND TONGUES AND DISCARDED THE REST. WHEN WE GOT TO THE HEART, MY MOTHER CUT OUT AND DISCARDED THE CHOKE, SLICED THE HEART INTO PIECES, AND DISTRIBUTED THE FLAVORFUL PIECES AMONG US FOR THE FINAL DIPPING. GOOD FRESH ARTICHOKES ARE HARD TO FIND IN MANY PARTS OF AMERICA, BUT IF YOU COME ACROSS THEM, TRY THEM IN THIS MOST SIMPLE AND DELICIOUS WAY. IN THE MEANWHILE, START OFF WITH SWEET FRESH FENNEL.

✳ 1 fennel bulb
✳ ½ cup extra-virgin olive oil
✳ salt and freshly milled black pepper

❶ TRIM OFF ANY BROWN or discolored spots from the fennel bulb. Cut off only a thin slice at the base of the bulb, because the base is needed to hold the overlapping stalks together once they are cut. Trim off most of the darker upper stalks and feathery leaves; reserve some of the trimmed leaves. Cut the bulb in half lengthwise, then cut each half into quarters lengthwise. You should have 8 long wedges.

❷ ARRANGE THE FENNEL WEDGES on a large plate. Pour the olive oil into a small dish, season with salt and pepper to taste, and place the bowl in the center of the plate for dipping. Chop some of the fennel leaves and sprinkle over the fennel wedges for garnish. Serve.

VERDURA ALLA GRIGLIA

GRILLED VEGETABLES

FOR 4 PEOPLE

DESPITE WHAT MIGHT SEEM LIKE A NOVEL IDEA TO MANY AMERICANS, GRILLING VEGETABLES IS AN ANCIENT PRACTICE IN ITALY AND OTHER PARTS OF THE MEDITERRANEAN. THERE ARE FEW VEGETABLES THAT ARE NOT SUPERB COOKED THIS WAY—TRANSFORMED BY THE SMOKY FLAVOR OF THE CHARCOAL GRILL INTO SOMETHING QUITE EXTRAORDINARY. IF A GRILL IS NOT PRACTICAL, THE VEGETABLES CAN BE PLACED ON A BAKING SHEET RUBBED WITH OLIVE OIL AND SUCCESSFULLY BROILED IN THE OVEN. AMONG MY FAVORITE VEGETABLES COOKED THIS WAY ARE ZUCCHINI, FENNEL, AND WILD MUSHROOMS. ❋ IN ITALY, WILD MUSHROOMS ARE OFTEN GRILLED AND DRIZZLED WITH GOOD OLIVE OIL, THEN SPRINKLED WITH SALT, PEPPER, AND PARSLEY. FRESH *porcini, cremini,* AND *portobello* MUSHROOMS, THE LAST TWO OF WHICH ARE BECOMING POPULAR IN SPECIALTY-PRODUCE MARKETS IN THE UNITED STATES, ARE DIFFICULT TO GRILL BECAUSE THEY CONTAIN LITTLE MOISTURE. THE MOST SUITABLE WILD MUSHROOMS FOR GRILLING ARE *shiitake* AND HEDGEHOG MUSHROOMS. EXPERIMENT WITH OTHER VARIETIES AS YOU FIND THEM. ❋ USE ANY OR ALL OF THE FOLLOWING VEGETABLES, OR TRY OTHERS OF YOUR OWN CHOOSING. BE SURE THAT ANY VEGETABLE YOU SELECT IS VERY FRESH.

about 2 pounds vegetables such as:
* *young eggplants*
* *young zucchini*
* *1 head* radicchio
* *1 fennel bulb*
* *whole fresh wild mushrooms such as* shiitake, chanterelle, *and/or hedgehog*

* *extra-virgin olive oil for oiling rack or baking sheet, basting, and drizzling*
* *salt and freshly milled black pepper*
* *chopped fresh Italian parsley for sprinkling on mushrooms (optional)*

❶ PREPARE A FIRE in a charcoal grill or preheat a broiler. Prepare the eggplants as directed for Deep-Fried Eggplant on page 20 through the draining and the wiping of the slices. Cut off the stems and navels from the zucchini and cut lengthwise into ⅛-inch-thick slices. Trim the base from the *radicchio* but leave the core intact. Cut the head lengthwise into 8 wedges. Cut the tubular stems off the fennel bulb and any outer tough stalks. Trim off any brown or discolored spots from the bulb. Cut off only a thin slice at the base of the bulb (the base is needed to hold the overlapping stalks together) and cut the bulb lengthwise into 8 wedges. Remove any dirt from the mushrooms with a soft brush or dry cotton towel. Trim off the hard tips of the stems.

❷ BRUSH THE VEGETABLES generously with olive oil on one side. Place them on an oiled grill or rack, or a baking sheet if you are broiling, oiled side up. Position the grill rack or broiler pan about 8 inches from the heat source; it must not be too close or the vegetables will burn. Grill or broil on both sides, using a metal spatula to flip them, until tender and nicely browned. Turn them only once and brush them on the second side with oil as soon as they are turned.

❸ ARRANGE THE VEGETABLES in an attractive way on a platter. Drizzle with additional extra-virgin olive oil and sprinkle to taste with salt and pepper. Sprinkle the mushrooms with parsley, if desired. Serve hot, warm, or at room temperature.

FUNGHI IN PADELLA ALL'AMENDOLARA

ANNA AMENDOLARA'S SAUTÉED MUSHROOMS

FOR 4 PEOPLE

❋

THIS STYLE OF SAUTÉING MUSHROOMS IS VERY MUCH IN THE MODE OF THE ITALIAN SOUTH. THE RECIPE WAS GIVEN TO ME BY ANNA AMENDOLARA NURSE, WHO COMES FROM APULIAN STOCK. THESE MUSHROOMS ARE A TERRIFIC *antipasto*, OR A LOVELY SIDE DISH WITH GRILLED LAMB CHOPS.

* 1 pound fresh white cultivated mushrooms
* ¼ cup extra-virgin olive oil
* ¼ cup fine dried bread crumbs
* 2 tablespoons chopped fresh Italian parsley
* 2 cloves garlic, finely chopped
* ¼ teaspoon dried oregano
* pinch of dried red-pepper flakes
* salt
* 1 lemon, cut into wedges

❶ REMOVE ANY DIRT from the mushrooms with a soft brush or dry cotton towel. Trim off the hard tips of the stems, but leave the stems attached. Cut the mushrooms lengthwise into quarters.

❷ HEAT THE OLIVE OIL over medium heat in a nonstick skillet that will easily accommodate the mushrooms without crowding them. Add the mushrooms as soon as the oil is hot enough to make them sizzle and sauté for 3 to 4 minutes, turning to brown all sides. Add the bread crumbs, parsley, garlic, oregano, and pepper flakes. Reduce the heat to medium-low and toss until the crumbs are golden brown, 3 to 4 minutes. Season to taste with salt. Serve with lemon wedges.

INSALATA DI PISELLI E MANDORLE

SUGAR SNAP PEA AND ALMOND SALAD WITH MINT AND ORANGE

FOR 4 PEOPLE

❋

FRESH SUGAR SNAP PEAS, MINT, ORANGE ZEST, AND ALMONDS COME TOGETHER TO CREATE THIS BEGUILING SALAD. SUGAR SNAP PEAS, WHICH ARE EATEN POD AND ALL, RETAIN THEIR SWEETNESS FAR LONGER THAN OTHER PEA VARIETIES THAT MUST BE SHELLED. BE SURE THEY ARE FRESH; THEY SHOULD NOT BE WRINKLED OR DULL LOOKING, BUT SHOULD BE A BRIGHT, SHINY GREEN. SUGAR SNAPS ARE ESPECIALLY SWEET, AND LIKE OTHER PEAS, THE FRESHER THEY ARE, THE SWEETER THEY ARE. THE MORE WIDELY AVAILABLE SNOW PEAS CAN BE SUBSTITUTED IF SUGAR SNAPS ARE UNAVAILABLE. IT IS IMPORTANT NOT TO OVERCOOK THE PEAS; THEY ARE MEANT TO BE COOKED VERY BRIEFLY, THEN REFRESHED IN COLD WATER SO THAT THEIR CRISP TEXTURE IS RETAINED.

* 2 teaspoons salt
* 1 pound sugar snap peas or snow peas, trimmed
* freshly milled white or black pepper
* 5 tablespoons slivered almonds, lightly toasted
* 2-½ tablespoons extra-virgin olive oil
* 5 tablespoons freshly squeezed orange juice, preferably from a blood orange
* 6 to 8 fresh mint or basil leaves, torn into small pieces

❶ BRING A SAUCEPAN FILLED WITH WATER to a boil. Add the salt first, then the peas, and boil, uncovered, for 1-½ minutes. Drain, immediately plunge them into cold water to stop further cooking, and drain again.

❷ PLACE THE PEAS in a salad bowl and add pepper to taste, almonds, olive oil, orange juice, and mint or basil. Toss well and serve. This salad will stay crisp for several hours at room temperature.

PEPERONI RIPIENI DI RISO E SALSICCIA

PEPPERS STUFFED WITH RICE AND SAUSAGE

FOR 8 PEOPLE

❊

ALMOST ANY VEGETABLE CAN BE STUFFED, BUT PEPPERS ARE PARTICULARLY SUITABLE BECAUSE OF THEIR CONTAINER-LIKE SHAPE. THIS IS HOW VEGETABLES ARE STUFFED IN GERMAN-SPEAKING ITALY'S TRENTINO–ALTO ADIGE, WHERE THEY ARE CALLED *gefülltes gemüse* IN THE LOCAL DIALECT.

* ⅓ cup extra-virgin olive oil
* 8 bell peppers, a mixture of red and yellow
* 1 onion, thinly sliced
* 1-¼ cups long-grain white rice
* 1-¾ cups plus 3 tablespoons full-flavored chicken, beef, or veal stock
* 1 teaspoon salt, or to taste
* ½ teaspoon freshly milled black pepper, or to taste
* 4 sweet Italian fennel sausages (about ¾ pound), casings removed and meat crumbled
* 2 ounces soppressata salame, cut into small dice
* 1 teaspoon fennel seed, pulverized in a spice grinder or in a mortar
* 2 tablespoons chopped fresh Italian parsley
* 2 tablespoons freshly grated parmigiano
* 1 large clove garlic, finely chopped
* 2 ounces mozzarella, cut into 8 same-sized cubes
* additional olive oil for oiling baking dish

❶ PREHEAT AN OVEN to 400 degrees F. In a large skillet over medium heat, warm the olive oil. Add the whole bell peppers and sauté until colored on all sides but still firm to the touch, 5 to 7 minutes. If they do not all fit into the pan at once, sauté them in batches to give them enough room to color properly. Remove from the heat and let cool. Slice the top off each pepper and reserve the tops. Scoop out and discard the seeds and ribs, being careful not to pierce the walls of the peppers, and set aside.

❷ DRAIN OFF ALL BUT 2 TABLESPOONS of the oil in the pan (reserve the drained oil) and place the pan over medium heat. Add the onion and sauté until it softens, about 5 minutes. Stir in the rice and sauté until translucent, about 5 minutes. Add the 1-¾ cups stock, salt, and pepper and bring to a boil. Immediately reduce the heat to a gentle simmer. Cover and cook until the liquid is absorbed and the rice is tender, about 10 minutes. Taste for salt.

❸ MEANWHILE, IN A SECOND SKILLET, sauté the sausage meat in a little of the oil reserved from browning the peppers (if necessary, use additional olive oil) until it colors but is not hard, 4 to 5 minutes. Add the cooked rice, soppressata, fennel, parsley, *parmigiano*, and garlic. Taste for salt and pepper. Remove from heat and allow to cool slightly. Fill the peppers with the rice mixture and insert a cube of *mozzarella* into the center of the stuffing. Replace the pepper tops.

❹ OIL A BAKING DISH ample enough to hold all the peppers without crowding them. Arrange the stuffed peppers in the dish upright and add the 3 tablespoons stock to the dish. Cover tightly with a lid or aluminum foil, dull side out, and bake in the oven until the peppers are tender but still hold their shape, about 30 minutes. Allow to settle for 10 to 15 minutes before serving. Serve hot or warm.

AHEAD-OF-TIME NOTE: This dish can be prepared up to the point where it goes into the oven 1 to 2 days in advance, or fully cooked 1 to 2 days in advance and then reheated. In either case, store, covered, in the refrigerator. To reheat, cover and place in an oven preheated to 350 degrees F for 30 minutes.

LEFT: Peperoni Ripieni di Salsiccia e Funghi (page 36)

PEPERONI RIPIENI DI SALSICCIA E FUNGHI

PEPPERS WITH FENNEL-FLAVORED BREAD, MUSHROOM, AND SAUSAGE STUFFING

FOR 6 PEOPLE

I OFFER A SECOND RECIPE FOR STUFFED PEPPERS BECAUSE THE TWO ARE MARKEDLY DIFFERENT FROM EACH OTHER. THIS ONE IS QUITE SWEET BECAUSE OF THE LARGE PROPORTION OF ONION AND FENNEL FLAVORING. AS WITH THE PRECEDING RECIPE, OTHER VEG-ETABLES—EGGPLANTS, ZUCCHINI, TOMATOES—CAN BE STUFFED AND BAKED WITH THIS LOVELY FILLING. (IF STUFFING EGGPLANTS OR ZUCCHINI, THE FLESH SHOULD BE SCOOPED OUT, CHOPPED, SALTED AND DRAINED, RINSED, SAUTÉED, AND ADDED TO THE STUFFING.)

* *6 yellow, orange, or red bell peppers, or a mixture*
* *3 tablespoons extra-virgin olive oil*
* *½ pound fresh white cultivated mushrooms*
* *3 tablespoons unsalted butter or extra-virgin olive oil*
* *1 onion, chopped*
* *1 teaspoon fennel seed, pulverized in a spice grinder or in a mortar*
* *salt and freshly milled black pepper*
* *4 sweet Italian fennel sausages (about ¾ pound), casings removed and meat crumbled*
* *¼ pound stale bread, cut into small dice*
* *½ to ¾ cup full-flavored chicken, veal, or beef stock for soaking bread, plus 3 table-spoons for baking the peppers*
* *2 tablespoons chopped fresh Italian parsley*
* *¼ cup freshly grated* parmigiano
* *additional olive oil for oiling baking dish*

❶ PREHEAT AN OVEN to 400 degrees F. In a large skillet over medium heat, warm the olive oil. Add the whole bell peppers and sauté until colored on all sides but still very firm, 5 to 7 minutes. Remove from the heat and let cool. Slice the top off of each pepper and reserve the tops. Scoop out and discard the seeds and ribs, being careful not to pierce the walls of the peppers, and set aside.

❷ REMOVE ANY DIRT from the mushrooms with a mushroom brush or dry cotton towel. Trim off the hard tips of the stems, then slice the mushrooms thinly. Set aside.

❸ In the same skillet over medium heat, warm the butter or olive oil. Add the onion and sauté gently until soft, about 5 minutes. Add the fennel, salt and pepper to taste, and sausage meat. Sauté until the meat colors but is not hard, about 4 to 5 minutes. Add the mushrooms and continue to sauté gently until soft, 3 to 4 minutes. Remove from the heat.

❹ In a small bowl, soak the bread in ½ to ¾ cup stock until it softens throughout. The amount of stock necessary will depend upon the hard-ness of the bread. The bread should be nicely moistened but not excessively wet. Add the soaked bread, parsley, and *parmigiano* to the sausage mixture and mix well. Season with salt and pepper. Fill the peppers with the sausage mixture and replace the tops.

❺ Oil a baking dish ample enough to hold all the peppers without crowding them. Arrange the stuffed peppers in the dish upright and add the 3 tablespoons stock. Cover tightly with a lid or aluminum foil, dull side out, and bake until the peppers are tender but still hold their shape, about 30 minutes. Allow to settle for 10 to 15 minutes before serving. Serve hot or warm.

AHEAD-OF-TIME NOTE: This dish can be prepared 1 to 2 days in advance, up to the point where it goes into the oven, or fully cooked 1 to 2 days in advance and then reheated. In either case, store, covered, in the refrigerator. To reheat, cover, and place in an oven preheated to 350 degrees F for 30 minutes.

INSALATA DI MELANZANE E PEPERONI ARROSTITI

ROASTED EGGPLANT, PEPPER, AND ONION SALAD

FOR 4 PEOPLE

❋

HERE IS A ROBUST AND COLORFUL ROASTED VEGETABLE DISH I DEVISED WHEN I WAS HANKERING AFTER THE FAMOUS SWEET-AND-SOUR SICILIAN APPETIZER, *caponata*, BUT DID NOT HAVE THE TIME TO MAKE IT. THE SWEETNESS COMES FROM THE NATURAL FLAVORS OF THE PEPPERS AND ONION; IT IS FOILED BEAUTIFULLY BY THE SALTINESS OF THE OLIVES AND CAPERS, AND THE SWEET-TART NATURE OF THE BALSAMIC VINEGAR. UNLIKE *caponata*, IN WHICH THE VEGETABLES ARE SAUTÉED, HERE THEY ARE ROASTED, WITH THE RESULT THAT THIS IS A LIGHTER DISH.

* *vegetable oil for oiling baking sheets*
* *3 young eggplants (about 1-½ pounds total weight), cut in half lengthwise*
* *1 large red bell pepper*
* *1 large yellow bell pepper*
* *1 large onion, unpeeled and halved*
* *1 small clove garlic, finely chopped or passed through a garlic press*
* *1 tablespoon chopped fresh Italian parsley*
* *1 tablespoon drained small capers or coarsely chopped large capers*
* *2 tablespoons extra-virgin olive oil*
* *1 tablespoon balsamic vinegar*
* *1 tablespoon sharp-flavored green olives, pitted and sliced*

❶ PREHEAT AN OVEN to 400 degrees F. Rub 2 baking sheets with vegetable oil. Place the eggplant halves, whole peppers, and onion halves on the baking sheets and roast in the preheated oven until the vegetables are tender, 25 to 30 minutes. Leave the eggplants and onion in one position throughout the cooking, but turn the peppers to expose on all sides so that they cook evenly.

❷ REMOVE FROM THE OVEN. When the peppers are cool enough to handle, peel off the skins using your fingertips, cut the peppers in half lengthwise, and remove and discard the stems, ribs, and seeds. Cut the peppers into long strips about 1-½-inches wide. If the eggplants have excessive seeds, remove them as well, along with the stems and navels. Leave their skins on, however, and cut the eggplants into strips approximately the same size as the pepper strips. Peel the onion halves and cut them into ½-inch dice.

❸ IN AN ATTRACTIVE SERVING BOWL, combine the cut vegetables. Add the garlic, parsley, capers, olive oil, vinegar, and olives and toss well. Serve warm, at room temperature, or chilled.

AHEAD-OF-TIME NOTE: This dish can be prepared 2 days in advance, covered, and refrigerated.

FUNGHI FARCITI

STUFFED MUSHROOMS

FOR 2 PEOPLE

Cultivated or wild mushrooms are suitable for this recipe, although wild mushrooms have more flavor. If using cultivated mushrooms, it is best to select those that are about two inches in diameter. White button mushrooms or the firmer, more tasty *cremini* (or *crimini*), also known as Italian, Roman, *prataoli*, brown, or field mushrooms, will do. *Portobello* mushrooms are simply *cremini* that have been allowed to grow larger. The *cremini*, which are cultivated mushrooms, are similiar to white button mushrooms in shape, but have beige bases and soft, brown caps. Numerous wild varieties can be used, although they must have the classic cap-and-stem shape, such as *porcini* do. Fresh *porcini* are rare in American markets, but *cremini* and *portobello* mushrooms have become quite common.

✳ *6 fresh porcini, cremini, or portobello mushrooms or cultivated mushrooms (about ½ pound total weight), each about 2 inches in diameter*

For the stuffing:
✳ *1 tablespoon fine dried bread crumbs*
✳ *1 tablespoon chopped fresh Italian parsley*
✳ *3 tablespoons chopped pancetta or lean bacon*
✳ *1-½ tablespoons extra-virgin olive oil*
✳ *2 tablespoons freshly grated parmigiano*
✳ *½ teaspoon chopped fresh rosemary, or ¼ teaspoon dried rosemary*
✳ *¼ teaspoon chopped fresh sage, or ⅛ teaspoon dried sage*
✳ *1 small clove garlic, finely chopped or passed through a garlic press*
✳ *¼ teaspoon salt*
✳ *freshly milled black pepper*
✳ *1 to 2 tablespoons milk, or as needed*

✳ *extra-virgin olive oil for oiling the dish*
✳ *dry white wine or vermouth for sprinkling*

❶ Preheat an oven to 400 degrees F. Remove any dirt from the mushrooms with a soft brush or dry cotton towel. Trim off the hard tips of the stems, then remove the stems and chop them. In a small bowl, combine the chopped stems with all the stuffing ingredients, including pepper to taste and enough milk to bind the mixture. Stir together thoroughly.

❷ Select a baking dish large enough to hold the mushrooms in a single layer and rub it lightly with olive oil. Divide the stuffing evenly among the mushroom caps, patting each portion into a nice, evenly rounded mound. Place the stuffed caps in the baking dish, stuffing side up, and sprinkle lightly with wine. Cover loosely with aluminum foil, dull side out, and bake in the preheated oven until the mushrooms are sizzling hot, 20 to 30 minutes. Serve hot or warm.

Variation: Add 6 sharp-flavored black olives, pitted and finely chopped, to the stuffing.

INSALATA DI CAVOLFIORE

CAULIFLOWER SALAD

FOR 6 PEOPLE

THIS ZESTY SALAD OF CAULIFLOWER IS TYPICAL OF THE SOUTH OF ITALY. IT OFTEN CONTAINS CHOPPED ANCHOVY AS WELL. I LIKE THE WAY THE TARTNESS OF THE OLIVES, CAPERS, AND LEMON PLAY OFF AGAINST THE EARTHINESS OF THE CAULIFLOWER, SO I PREFER NOT TO MUDDLE THE FLAVORS WITH THE ADDITION OF ANCHOVIES. THIS IS A MATTER OF TASTE, HOWEVER. THE FRUITY EXTRA-VIRGIN OLIVE OIL ROUNDS OUT THE ZESTY FLAVORS OF THE OTHER INGREDIENTS.

* *1 large head cauliflower*
* *1 tablespoon salt*
* *juice of ½ lemon*

FOR THE DRESSING:
* *12 sharp-flavored black olives, pitted and thinly sliced*
* *1 tablespoon drained small capers or coarsely chopped large capers*
* *1 teaspoon whole fresh thyme leaves, or ½ teaspoon dried thyme*
* *¼ cup extra-virgin olive oil, or to taste*
* *3 tablespoons freshly squeezed lemon juice*
* *salt and freshly milled black pepper*

❶ POUR ENOUGH WATER into a saucepan to cover the cauliflower generously and bring to a boil. Meanwhile, trim the stalks off the cauliflower and cut off the hard base and discard. Cut the cauliflower into quarters lengthwise. Add the cauliflower to the boiling water, along with the salt and lemon juice (the lemon juice will help the cauliflower to retain its color). Cover, return to a boil, and continue to cook until the cauliflower is tender but not mushy, 5 to 7 minutes. Take care, as cauliflower goes from undercooked to overcooked very quickly.

❷ MEANWHILE, IN A SMALL BOWL combine all the dressing ingredients, including salt and pepper to taste. Whisk to blend.

❸ WHEN THE CAULIFLOWER IS COOKED, drain, immediately plunge it into cold water to stop further cooking, and drain again. Allow to cool, then break up into quite small florets so that the cauliflower will combine easily with the dressing, and place in a salad bowl. (If the florets are too large, the olives and capers will fall to the bottom of the salad bowl.) Pour the dressing over the top, toss well, and serve.

VARIATION: Add 10 anchovy fillets in olive oil, drained and coarsely chopped, to the dressing.

CHAPTER 3

EGGS, CROQUETTES, & FRITTERS

• • •

Uova, crocchette, e frittelle

DESPITE a certain prowess in the kitchen, I have never been able to make a decent omelet. Even Bob, my husband, who cannot cook anything else, can make a spectacular one. I suspect his skill at flipping eggs is a by-product of some romantic liaison during his bachelor days in France. I, on the other hand, was inspired by my mother's way with eggs, the Italian way, and I suppose that her hand is behind every miscooked omelet I've made, trying to turn it into a *frittata* instead. ❋ In her marvelous classic cookbook, *Italian Food,* the English writer Elizabeth David begins the chapter on egg cookery by saying "it must be admitted that very few Italian cooks have the right touch with egg dishes. They are particularly stubborn with regard to the cooking of omelettes...." She objects in particular to the *frittata,* which she characterizes as a misbegotten omelet: "[The Italians] use far too much of the filling . . . in proportion to the number of eggs," she continues, "and in consequence produce a pudding rather than an omelette." ❋ It must be understood that the Italian *frittata*–literally, "fried dish"– is not an omelet at all. It is a kind of *sformato,* or "mold," of eggs and anything from herbs and vegetables to ham, sausage, meat, seafood, cheese, pasta, potatoes, or rice. *Frittata* are firm not runny, and when turned out of the pan, they resemble a low, flat cake rather than the puffy crescent of the classic French omelet. Unlike an omelet, which is flavored with herbs or what have you but not dominated by them, the filling in a *frittata* is at least as important as the eggs. ❋ Other popular egg dishes in the *antipasto* category include stuffed hard-cooked eggs, for which there are many delicious fillings, and *frittatine,* small, thin *frittata* that can be stuffed and rolled. No recipes for the latter are given in these pages, but fillings for *frittatine* can include slices of *prosciutto* or *salame,* cheese, or more elaborate combinations such as *béchamel* sauce and mushrooms, asparagus, shrimp, or ham. ❋ Croquettes and fritters have typically, although not always, been vehicles for leftover foods. There are many varieties, some of which appear as *antipasti* or as snack foods in *rosticcerie,* the Italian take-out shops. Some are made from cooked, chopped, and seasoned vegetables such as green beans, which are then deep-fried in olive oil. Dried beans and

chick-peas (*ceci*) may also be treated in this way. Such a dish is the rustic *polpettine di fagioli* of Trentino, deep-fried croquettes of puréed cooked *borlotti* beans, onion, parsley, egg, and bread crumbs. Cooked leftover meats are often turned into croquettes such as in the *mondeghili* of Lombardy, which include grated cheese, herbs, and beaten egg. One of the tastiest croquettes, typical of Liguria, is that made of dried fish, salt cod (*baccalà*) in particular. The many variations of these croquettes and fritters reflect the lay of the land as well as regional traditions, and are too numerous to include in this chapter, but I offer a few of my favorites. ❊ All croquettes and fritters contain either *béchamel* sauce or eggs, which serve to bind the mixture together so that it does not disintegrate when fried. The most famous of all these specialties are probably those made of rice. In *Guida all'Italia gastronomica,* Massimo Alberini and Giorgio Mistretta state that rice croquettes originated in Sicily, where they are called *arancini.* These are made by combining rice with a meat *ragù* and sometimes peas. *Mozzarella* or another soft cheese is inserted into the middle. In Rome, similar rice croquettes are made with a tomato-flavored *risotto* and *mozzarella* tucked inside. They are called *supplí al telefono* because when bitten into while piping hot, the cheese oozes out and forms stringy "telephone lines" between croquette and mouth. I prefer these simpler rice croquettes of Rome, which my mother has always made, and for which her recipe is included. ❊ ❊ ❊

FRITTATE: open-faced omelets. When I was growing up, my mother always made *frittate* of fresh artichokes, zucchini, or red bell peppers. They were delicious and beautifully colored, the sunny yellow of the eggs and the mosaic of vivid vegetable colors forming a lovely terrazzolike palette. ❊ The *frittata* has a long history in Italy.

Portable, economical, nourishing, and delicious cold, vegetable frittata between two slabs of bread has for centuries been the traditional lunch of the laborer. But it has not been confined to the workplace table. It is a popular *antipasto,* or in combination with a few vegetable *antipasti,* it makes a perfect lunch or light supper. ❊ A *frittata* always tastes best served warm, at room temperature, or cold–never hot. The filling and the eggs need time to settle after cooking, and the flavors of all the ingredients merge and intensify as the *frittata* cools. ❊ While the *frittata* is an uncomplicated dish to make, there are a few things that should be kept in mind in its preparation. Vegetable fillings should not be too watery: zucchini should be drained after cooking; spinach and chard should be squeezed dry before being chopped and added to the eggs. *Frittate* should never be overcooked, or they become dry and brittle. For this reason, it is important to cook them over gentle heat and to be sure to use a heavy-bottomed skillet or omelet pan to prevent them from cooking too quickly. It is also important to oil the pan sufficiently to allow the *frittata* to slip out easily when it is done. ❊ There are two ways to brown the top of a *frittata.* I find that it is easiest to slip it under a preheated broiler for one to two minutes. Alternatively, loosen the edges of the cooked *frittata* from the pan sides with a spatula, invert a dish on top of the pan, and immediately invert the pan so that the *frittata* rests on the dish. Then slide the *frittata* back into the pan and cook until browned on the bottom, one to two minutes. Finally, loosen the edges once again and invert onto a plate to serve. ❊ *Frittate* can be refrigerated successfully and served the following day, chilled or at room temperature. ❊ ❊ ❊

CROCCHETTE DI RISO

RICE CROQUETTES

FOR 5 PEOPLE

THESE RICE BALLS ARE POPULAR THROUGHOUT ITALY AND GO BY DIFFERENT NAMES: *suppli' al telefono* IN ROME, *arancini* IN SICILY, AND, IN GENERAL, *crocchette di riso.* I AM PARTIAL TO THOSE THAT CONTAIN TOMATO SAUCE; *MOZZARELLA* GOES SO WELL WITH TOMATO, AND I THINK THAT THEY ARE MORE TASTY THAN THE NONTOMATO VARIATIONS. I HAVE FOUND THE MOST SUCCESSFUL METHOD FOR MAKING THESE DELICIOUS CROQUETTES IS FIRST TO COOK A *risotto* RATHER THAN SIMPLY TO BOIL THE RICE. (ITALIANS TYPICALLY COOK EXTRA *risotto* FOR MAKING CROQUETTES THE NEXT DAY WITH THE "LEFTOVERS.") IT PRODUCES BALLS THAT HOLD TOGETHER WELL, BECAUSE THE RICE, HAVING ABSORBED STOCK AND CHEESE, IS STICKIER (AS WELL AS TASTIER). *Risotto* IS A SIMPLE DISH TO MAKE IF THESE RULES ARE REMEMBERED: USE AUTHENTIC ITALIAN ARBORIO RICE (LONG-GRAIN RICE CAN BE SUBSTITUTED, BUT IT WILL NOT PRODUCE AS CREAMY A *risotto*), BE SURE THE STOCK IS HOT (COLD LIQUID WILL BRING DOWN THE TEMPERATURE), AND ADD THE STOCK A LADLEFUL AT A TIME UNTIL IT IS ABSORBED INTO THE RICE BEFORE ADDING MORE.

FOR THE *risotto:*
* 3 tablespoons unsalted butter or extra-virgin olive oil
* ½ small onion, grated
* 1 cup Arborio rice
* 1-½ cups Neapolitan-Style Tomato Sauce (page 129) or leftover tomato sauce or ragù (tomato-meat sauce)
* 2-¼ cups full-flavored chicken or beef stock, heated
* ¼ cup freshly grated parmigiano
* salt
* freshly milled black pepper
* 1 whole egg, plus 1 egg yolk, well beaten

* ½ pound mozzarella, cut into ½-inch cubes
* olive oil for deep-frying
* 1 egg white, lightly beaten
* about ½ cup fine dried bread crumbs for coating

❶ FOR THE *risotto,* in a heavy skillet over medium heat, melt the butter or warm the oil. Add the onion and sauté until softened, about 2 minutes. Add the rice and sauté for several minutes until well coated. Stir in the sauce. When it is absorbed, add a ladleful of the hot stock, stirring well. When it is nearly completely absorbed into the rice, add an additional ladleful of the stock. Continue cooking as described, adding a ladleful of hot stock at a time and then stirring until it is absorbed before adding the next ladleful. When the stock is used up (the rice should be tender but not mushy), remove the rice from the heat and stir in the *parmigiano.* Season to taste with salt and pepper. Allow the *risotto* to cool to room temperature, then stir in the whole egg and egg yolk. Cover and chill for at least 2 hours or overnight.

❷ FORM SPOONFULS of the chilled *risotto* into log shapes about 2 inches long and 1 inch thick, stuffing the center of each with a few pieces of the diced *mozzarella* (the croquettes should not be too large). You should have about 15 croquettes in all.

❸ POUR THE OLIVE OIL into a deep skillet to a depth of about 2 inches. Heat to 350 degrees F, or until a crust of bread turns golden within seconds of being dropped into it. Just before frying each croquette, dip it into the egg white, then roll it in the bread crumbs. (The croquettes should not be rolled in the crumbs until the last minute, or they will not be properly crisp when fried.) Carefully slip the croquettes into the hot oil. Do not crowd the pan or the temperature of the oil will drop. Fry until golden on all sides, just a few minutes. Remove with a slotted utensil to paper towels to drain. Keep them in a warm oven while you fry the remaining croquettes. Serve piping hot.

AHEAD-OF-TIME NOTE: The croquettes can be made in advance, covered and refrigerated for 1 to 2 days, and then reheated in an oven preheated to 350 degrees F before serving.

SFORMATO DI TONNO E PATATE

COLD TUNA AND POTATO LOAF

FOR 6 PEOPLE

A *sformato* IS A MOLDED DISH, SERVED EITHER HOT OR COLD. THIS *sformato* IS A DISH FROM MY CHILDHOOD, ONE OF MANY COLD *ANTIPASTI* MY MOTHER PREPARED IN THE SUMMER. NIKA HAZELTON DESCRIBES A SIMILAR DISH FROM TUSCANY IN *The Regional Italian Kitchen.* ❋ EXCEPT FOR THE MASHED POTATOES, THIS DISH REQUIRES NO COOKING. IT CAN EASILY BE MADE A DAY OR TWO, OR EVEN THREE IN ADVANCE OF EATING. CUCUMBERS AND WATERCRESS AND A HARD-COOKED EGG OR TWO ARE THE PERFECT GARNISH.

❋ *1 recipe Light Lemon Mayonnaise (page 127)*
❋ *1 pound Idaho potatoes or waxy boiling potatoes*
❋ *2 tablespoons unsalted butter, at room temperature*
❋ *6 tablespoons milk or light or heavy cream*
❋ *2 cans (6-½ ounces each) imported Italian light tuna in olive oil, partially drained*
❋ *¼ cup freshly grated parmigiano*
❋ *⅛ teaspoon freshly grated nutmeg*
❋ *2 tablespoons chopped fresh Italian parsley*
❋ *2 tablespoons very finely chopped or grated red onion*
❋ *½ teaspoon salt, or to taste*
❋ *freshly milled black pepper*
❋ *1 tablespoon drained small capers*
❋ *thinly sliced cucumber and watercress or soft lettuce for garnish*
❋ *2 eggs, hard-cooked and sliced, for garnish (optional)*

❶ MAKE THE MAYONNAISE, cover, and chill.

❷ SELECT A FISH-SHAPED MOLD or a bowl with about a 4-cup capacity. Rinse it with cold water and place it in the freezer for at least 30 minutes.

❸ MEANWHILE, place the unpeeled potatoes in a pot with cold water to cover and bring to a boil over high heat. Immediately reduce the heat to medium and cook until tender when pierced with a cake tester or sharp knife, about 20 minutes. Drain and, when cool enough to handle but still hot, peel them and pass them through a potato ricer or food mill or mash them with a potato masher. Return them to the pot and, using a wooden spoon, beat in the butter and milk or cream.

❹ IN A LARGE BOWL, finely flake the tuna with a fork. Add the potatoes, ¼ cup of the mayonnaise, the cheese, nutmeg, parsley, onion, salt, and pepper to taste and mix well. Remove the mold or bowl from the freezer and spoon the mixture into it, pressing it a bit in order to pack it well. Cover with plastic wrap and refrigerate for 4 hours or overnight.

❺ INVERT THE *sformato* onto a dish or platter and lift off the mold. Using a small spatula or butter knife, smooth some mayonnaise over the *sformato,* just as you would spread icing on a cake. (Reserve some of the mayonnaise to spread on the hard-cooked eggs, if you are using them, and for serving.) Sprinkle with the capers. Garnish with cucumber, watercress or lettuce, and the egg slices, if using. Pass the remaining mayonnaise at the table.

FRITTATA DI BIETOLE O SPINACI

FRITTATA WITH SWISS CHARD OR SPINACH

FOR 4 TO 6 PEOPLE

SWISS CHARD IS NOT AS WELL-KNOWN TO US AS SPINACH, BUT IT IS WORTH TRYING IN A *frittata* FOR ITS DELICATE, SWEET FLAVOR THAT HARMONIZES SO NICELY WITH EGGS. IT HAS MORE BODY THAN SPINACH WHEN COOKED, SO WILL HAVE MORE OF A PRESENCE IN THE TEXTURE OF THE FINISHED DISH. WHETHER USING CHARD OR SPINACH, THE METHOD IS THE SAME.

* *1 pound Swiss chard or spinach, stemmed*
* *3 tablespoons extra-virgin olive oil*
* *1 onion, thinly sliced*
* *6 eggs*
* *2 tablespoons freshly grated parmigiano*
* *pinch of freshly grated nutmeg*
* *2 teaspoons chopped fresh thyme, or*
  1 teaspoon dried thyme
* *½ teaspoon salt*
* *freshly milled black pepper*

❶ P**REHEAT A BROILER.** Place the chard or spinach in a saucepan without the addition of any more water than the drops still clinging to the leaves from washing. Cover and cook over medium heat until the leaves wilt and are tender; just a few minutes. Remove from the heat and let cool. Then using your hands squeeze out as much water as you can. Chop coarsely and set aside.

❷ I**N A SMALL SKILLET OVER MEDIUM-LOW HEAT,** warm 1 tablespoon of the olive oil. Add the onion and sauté until golden, 6 to 8 minutes. Remove from the heat and let cool slightly.

❸ M**EANWHILE,** in a bowl, beat the eggs lightly with a fork. Beat in the cheese, nutmeg, thyme, chard or spinach, salt, and pepper to taste. When the onion is cool enough not to cook the eggs, stir it into the mixture.

❹ P**OUR THE REMAINING** 2 tablespoons olive oil into a flameproof 12-inch skillet or omelet pan and place over medium heat. When it is hot enough to make the eggs sizzle, add the egg mixture, using a fork or spoon to distribute the vegetable evenly. Immediately reduce the heat to low and cook until the *frittata* is set but not browned, 12 to 15 minutes. Take care not to overcook the eggs or they will lose their delicacy.

❺ T**O FINISH COOKING,** slide the pan under the preheated broiler 6 inches from the heat until the top is golden, 1 to 2 minutes. Using a spatula to loosen the edges from the pan, slide the *frittata* out onto a serving plate. Serve warm or cold, cut into wedges.

FRITTATA DI ZUCCHINE

ZUCCHINI FRITTATA

FOR 4 TO 6 PEOPLE

❉

HERE IS A TRULY LOVELY SUMMER DISH. THE COOKED ZUCCHINI AND ONION MAKE THIS *frittata* DELIGHTFULLY SWEET.

* *4 tablespoons extra-virgin olive oil*
* *1 large onion, coarsely chopped*
* *1 teaspoon fresh thyme, chopped,*
  or ½ teaspoon dried thyme
* *1-½ pounds young, firm zucchini*
  (preferably no more than 6 ounces each)
* *2 tablespoons chopped fresh basil*
  or Italian parsley
* *5 extra-large eggs*
* *½ teaspoon salt*
* *freshly milled black pepper*
* *½ cup freshly grated* parmigiano, *or a*
  mixture of parmigiano *and* pecorino

❶ PREHEAT A BROILER. In a small skillet over medium heat, warm 2 tablespoons of the olive oil. Add the onion and the dried thyme, if using, and sauté until the onion wilts, about 5 minutes. Meanwhile, cut off the stems and navels from the zucchini, cut them in half lengthwise, and then cut them crosswise into thin slices. Add the zucchini, cover, and cook over medium heat, stirring a few times, until tender but not mushy, 10 to 12 minutes. Just before the zucchini slices are done, add the fresh thyme, if using, and the basil or parsley. Place the mixture in a colander to cool and to allow excess water to drain out, about 10 minutes.

❷ MEANWHILE, IN A BOWL, beat the eggs lightly with a fork. Beat in the salt, pepper to taste, and cheese. Add the drained cooled zucchini and onion.

❸ POUR THE REMAINING 2 tablespoons olive oil in a flameproof 12-inch skillet or omelet pan and place over medium heat. When it is hot enough to make the eggs sizzle, pour in the egg mixture, using a fork or spoon to distribute the zucchini evenly. Immediately reduce the heat to low and cook the *frittata* gently until it is set, 12 to 15 minutes. Take care not to overcook the eggs or they will lose their delicacy.

❹ TO FINISH COOKING, slide the pan under the preheated broiler 6 inches from the heat until the top is golden, 1 to 2 minutes. Using a spatula to loosen the edges from the pan, slide the *frittata* out onto a serving plate. Serve warm or cold, cut into wedges.

FRITTELLE DI PATATE CON FUNGHI TRIFOLATI E LA FONDUTA

POTATO FRITTERS WITH SAUTÉED WILD MUSHROOMS AND FONTINA CHEESE SAUCE

FOR 5 PEOPLE

THE COMBINATION OF POTATO FRITTERS, SAUTÉED *porcini,* AND *fonduta,* A HOT, THICK, VELVETY CHEESE "DIP" MADE FROM *fontina,* IS A CREATION OF PIEDMONTESE CHEF ROBERT DONNA WHO SERVES THE DISH IN HIS WASHINGTON-BASED RESTAURANTS, GALILEO AND I MATTI TRATTORIA. *Fonduta,* A SPECIALITY OF PIEDMONT, IS TRADITIONALLY SERVED STEAMING HOT IN A POT OVER A BURNER. DINERS DIP CUBES OF TOASTED BREAD IMPALED ONTO LONG FORKS INTO THE CREAMY MIXTURE.

FOR THE *fonduta:*
* 5 ounces fontina *cheese, crust removed and diced*
* 1 cup milk
* 4 tablespoons unsalted butter
* 2 egg yolks

FOR THE *frittelle:*
* 14 ounces Idaho potatoes
* 2 eggs, beaten
* pinch of freshly grated nutmeg
* salt
* freshly milled black pepper
* olive oil for deep-frying
* all-purpose flour for dredging

FOR THE MUSHROOMS:
* 10 ounces fresh or frozen porcini, or 12 ounces other fresh wild mushrooms (see introduction)
* 3 tablespoons extra-virgin olive oil
* 2 large cloves garlic, bruised
* 2 tablespoons chopped fresh Italian parsley
* salt and freshly milled black pepper

* white truffle shavings (optional)

❶ THREE TO SIX HOURS before you want to serve the *frittelle,* make the *fonduta.* Place the cheese in a bowl, cover it with the milk, and leave for at least 3 hours and up to 6 hours at room temperature. Fifteen minutes to half an hour before serving, melt the butter in the top pan of a double boiler over gently boiling water. Be sure that the pan bottom is not touching the boiling water or the eggs will curdle when they are added. Add the *fontina* and milk and heat until the cheese melts, stirring once or twice. Whisk in the egg yolks and cook over low heat, whisking occasionally, until the mixture is creamy, 20 to 30 minutes. Cover the pot and keep the *fonduta* warm, but be careful not to cook it further, or the cheese will become stringy.

❷ FOR THE *frittelle,* preheat an oven to 450 degrees F. Place the potatoes slightly apart from each other directly on the oven rack (do not wrap them in aluminum foil). Bake until tender, about 1 hour for large potatoes, 50 minutes for medium potatoes, and 45 minutes for small potatoes. Use a cake tester or sharp knife to test for doneness. Remove from the oven and let cool until they can be handled, then peel them and pass them through a potato ricer or food mill into a bowl (never use a food processor; it will turn the potatoes into a gummy mess). Add the eggs, nutmeg, and salt and pepper to taste and mix well. Allow the mixture to sit for 10 minutes.

❸ PREHEAT AN OVEN to 200 degrees F. Form the potato mixture into thin 2-inch patties; you should have 15 patties in all. Pour the olive oil into a deep skillet to a depth of about 2 inches. Heat to 350 degrees F, or until a crust of bread turns golden within seconds of being dropped into it. Dredge the patties lightly in flour, then carefully slip them into the oil. Do not crowd the pan or the temperature of the oil will drop. Turn the patties in the oil and fry until golden on both sides, just a few minutes. Remove with a slotted utensil to paper towels to drain and place on a serving dish. Keep them in a warm oven while you fry the remaining patties, and then sauté the mushrooms.

❹ TO PREPARE THE MUSHROOMS, remove any grit with a soft brush or a dry cotton towel. Trim off the hard tips of the stems and any other woody parts. Cut into slices about 1/4 inch thick. In a large skillet that will give the mushrooms plenty of room, pour in the olive oil and add the garlic. Turn the heat to medium-low, and sauté the garlic until golden, about 5 minutes. Remove and discard the garlic before it turns brown. Turn the heat to high and add the mushrooms, parsley, and salt and pepper to taste and sauté briefly to sear the mushrooms. Keep warm.

❺ TO SERVE, place 3 tablespoons of *fonduta* on each serving dish. Place 3 *frittelle* in the middle and cover each with a spoonful of the sautéed mushrooms.

AHEAD-OF-TIME NOTE: The *fonduta* can be prepared 1 or 2 days in advance and refrigerated. When ready to serve, heat it carefully in the top pan of a double boiler over, but not in, gently boiling water. Allow it to heat through, but not come to a simmer. The *frittelle* can be made 1 day in advance up to the point where they are formed into patties. Cover and refrigerate the patties until you are ready to fry them.

CROCCHETTE DI TONNO E PATATE

TUNA AND POTATO CROQUETTES

FOR 5 OR 6 PEOPLE

❋

TUNA AND POTATOES ARE A CLASSIC COMBINATION IN ITALIAN COOKING AND THEY ARE ESPECIALLY COMPATIBLE IN THESE CROQUETTES. CANNED IMPORTED LIGHT TUNA IN OLIVE OIL IS AN EXCELLENT PRODUCT, ONE OF THE FEW CANNED FOODS, OTHER THAN PLUM TOMATOES AND ANCHOVIES, FOR WHICH NO APOLOGIES NEED BE MADE. DO NOT ASSUME THAT ALL TUNA BRANDS ARE EQUAL, HOWEVER. IMPORTED ITALIAN LIGHT TUNA IN OLIVE OIL IS VERY DIFFERENT IN FLAVOR FROM WHITE ALBACORE TUNA. IT IS FROM THE BELLY OF THE FISH, A PARTICULARLY MOIST, SWEET PART OF THE ANATOMY. PACKED IN OLIVE OIL, THIS BELLY TUNA RETAINS ITS MOISTURE AND ACQUIRES THE LOVELY FLAVOR OF THE OIL. YOU MAY NEED TO EXPERIMENT WITH DIFFERENT BRANDS OF IMPORTED TUNA. THE BEST BELLY TUNA IS PINK, NOT THE PALE BROWN OF INFERIOR LABELS. THE AMERICAN PREOCCUPATION WITH CALORIES HAS MADE WHITE ALBACORE TUNA PACKED IN WATER POPULAR, BUT THIS TUNA HAS VERY LITTLE FLAVOR AND A DRY MEALY TEXTURE THAT MAKES IT BOTH UNAPPETIZING AND UNSUITABLE FOR THIS RECIPE AND MANY OTHER ITALIAN RECIPES. ❋ THE PURÉED POTATO PROVIDES ENOUGH MOISTURE SO THAT NO *béchamel* OR OTHER SAUCE IS NECESSARY. THE ADDITION OF NUTMEG ADDS A WHISPER OF ELEGANCE TO THESE SIMPLE *antipasti*.

* *1 pound Idaho potatoes or waxy boiling potatoes*
* *2 tablespoons milk, warmed*
* *2 whole eggs*
* *2 cans (6-½ ounces each) imported Italian light tuna in olive oil, drained and flaked*
* *2 tablespoons freshly grated* parmigiano
* *1 tablespoon chopped fresh Italian parsley*
* *¾ teaspoon freshly grated nutmeg*
* *1½ teaspoon salt*
* *½ teaspoon freshly milled black pepper*
* *olive oil for frying*
* *1 egg white, lightly beaten*
* *about ½ cup fine dried bread crumbs for coating*

❶ PUT THE UNPEELED POTATOES in a pot with enough cold water to cover and bring to a boil over high heat. Immediately reduce the heat to medium and cook until tender when pierced with a cake tester or a sharp knife, about 20 minutes. Drain, and when cool enough to handle but still hot, peel the potatoes and pass them through a potato ricer or a food mill into a large bowl. Stir in the milk, then mix in the whole eggs, tuna, cheese, parsley, nutmeg, salt, and pepper. Using about 1 tablespoon for each croquette, form the mixture into small log shapes. You should have about 16 croquettes in all.

❷ POUR OLIVE OIL into a deep skillet to a depth of about half the height of the croquettes. Heat to 350 degrees F, or until a crust of bread turns golden within seconds of being dropped into it. Just before frying each croquette, dip it into the egg white, then roll it in the bread crumbs. (The croquettes should not be rolled in the crumbs until the last minute, or they will not be properly crisp when fried.) Carefully slip the croquettes into the hot oil. Do not crowd the pan or the temperature of the oil will drop. Fry until golden on all sides, just a few minutes. Remove with a slotted utensil to paper towels to drain. If you like, keep them piping hot in a warm oven while you fry the remaining croquettes. Serve hot or warm.

TORTINO DI MELANZANE E FUNGHI

EGGPLANT AND MUSHROOM FLAN

FOR 10 TO 12 PEOPLE

THE DIFFERENCE BETWEEN A *frittata* AND A *tortino* IS THAT THE LATTER USUALLY CONTAINS CREAM AND THUS RESEMBLES A FLAN MORE THAN AN OMELET. EGGPLANT AND MUSHROOMS ARE HIGHLY COMPATIBLE IN THIS DELICIOUS *tortino*.

✳ *1 large eggplant (1 ¼ to 1 ½ pounds)*
✳ *¼ pound fresh wild mushrooms such as oyster,* shiitake, *or* chanterelle
✳ *4 tablespoons extra-virgin olive oil*
✳ *1 large onion, thinly sliced*
✳ *salt to taste, plus ¾ teaspoon*
✳ *freshly milled black pepper*
✳ *4 eggs, lightly beaten*
✳ *1 cup light cream or heavy cream*
✳ *¼ cup freshly grated* parmigiano
✳ *1 teaspoon chopped fresh thyme, or ½ teaspoon dried thyme*
✳ *olive oil or unsalted butter for greasing baking dish*

❶ PEEL THE EGGPLANT and then prepare it as directed for Deep-Fried Eggplant on page 20 through the draining of the slices. Rinse and dry the eggplant slices well in a clean cotton towel. Cut the slices into lengthwise strips approximately 2 ½ inches long and 1 inch wide. Set aside.

❷ MEANWHILE, remove any dirt from the mushrooms with a soft brush or dry cotton towel. Trim off the hard tips of the stems, or cut off the whole stems if they are tough and woody. Slice the caps very thinly.

❸ PREHEAT AN OVEN to 350 degrees F. In a skillet (preferably nonstick) over medium heat, warm 2 tablespoons of the olive oil. Add the onion and sauté until wilted, about 5 minutes. Add the mushrooms and sauté gently until the mushrooms are tender, about 10 minutes. Transfer the mixture to a bowl.

❹ POUR THE REMAINING 2 tablespoons olive oil into the pan and add the eggplant. Stir to coat the pieces, cover, and cook over medium-low heat until tender, about 10 minutes. Stir occasionally to prevent sticking. Transfer to the bowl with the mushrooms and onion and season to taste with salt and pepper. Allow to cool.

❺ MEANWHILE, pass the beaten eggs through a fine-mesh sieve into a large bowl. Add the cream, cheese, ¾ teaspoon salt, pepper to taste, and thyme and beat with a fork or whisk. Stir in the eggplant mixture.

❻ RUB A 2-QUART BAKING DISH (9 by 12 inches or 7 by 11 inches and 1-½ to 2 inches deep) with olive oil or butter. Pour in the egg-vegetable mixture and place the *tortino* on the center rack of the preheated oven. Cover loosely with aluminum foil, dull side out, and bake until a cake tester or knife inserted in the center comes out clean, 35 to 40 minutes.

❼ REMOVE THE *tortino* from the oven and turn the oven to the broiler setting. Remove the foil and slip the *tortino* 8 inches under the broiler until golden, 3 to 4 minutes. Allow to settle for 20 to 30 minutes before serving. Serve warm or at room temperature.

FRITTATA DI CARCIOFI

ARTICHOKE FRITTATA

FOR 4 TO 6 PEOPLE

✳

BEING AN ARTICHOKE LOVER, THIS IS PROBABLY MY FAVORITE *frittata*. CLEANING ARTICHOKES IS SOMEWHAT TEDIOUS, BUT WELL WORTH THE TROUBLE. FROZEN, CANNED, OR BOTTLED ARTICHOKES DO NOT PRESERVE ANY OF THE VIRTUES OF FRESH ARTICHOKES, AND SHOULD NOT BE SUBSTITUTED.

* *1 tablespoon freshly squeezed lemon juice or vinegar*
* *3 artichokes (about 1/2 pound each)*
* *1 teaspoon salt*
* *4 tablespoons extra-virgin olive oil*
* *1 large onion, finely chopped*
* *6 extra-large eggs*
* *freshly milled black pepper*
* *3 tablespoons freshly grated* parmigiano
* *1 tablespoon chopped fresh marjoram, or 1 teaspoon dried marjoram*
* *2 tablespoons coarsely chopped fresh Italian parsley*

❶ PREHEAT A BROILER. Have ready a large ceramic bowl (do not use metal) filled with cold water to which you have added the lemon juice or vinegar. Trim only a thin slice from the bottom of the stem of each artichoke to remove the dark skin. Pare off all the green skin. The flesh of the stem is good. With your hand, pull off the tough outer leaves until you reach leaves that have tender, white areas at their base. Cut off only the upper part of the inner leaves that are dark green at the top and light greenish yellow at the base. The inner rows of leaves are the tender part you want, so be careful not to cut away too much. Cut the artichoke in half lengthwise and, with a small knife, cut out the hairy choke and any other tough inner purple leaves. Immediately put the cleaned artichokes into the acidulated water to prevent them from turning brown. When all of the artichokes have been trimmed, drain them. Place each artichoke half cut side down on a surface and cut lengthwise into ¼-inch-thick slices.

❷ Bring a large saucepan filled with water to a boil. Add the artichokes and ¾ teaspoon of the salt and boil until tender but not mushy. Fresh, young artichokes will be ready in approximately 5 minutes; old, tough artichokes may take up to 10 to 12 minutes. Drain and allow to cool.

❸ In a small skillet over medium heat, warm 2 tablespoons of the olive oil. Add the onion and sauté until golden, 6 to 8 minutes. Remove from the heat and let cool slightly.

❹ Meanwhile, in a bowl, beat the eggs lightly with a fork. Beat in the remaining ¼ teaspoon salt, pepper to taste, and cheese. Add the cooled artichokes, onion, and herbs.

❺ Pour the remaining 2 tablespoons olive oil into a flameproof 12-inch skillet or omelet pan and place over medium heat. When it is hot enough to make the eggs sizzle, add the egg mixture, using a fork or spoon to distribute the artichokes evenly. Immediately reduce the heat to low and cook over gentle heat until the *frittata* is set but not browned, 12 to 15 minutes. Take care not to overcook the eggs or they will lose their delicacy.

❻ To finish cooking, slide the pan under the preheated broiler 6 inches from the heat until the top is golden, 1 to 2 minutes. Using a spatula to loosen the edges from the pan, slide the *frittata* out onto a serving plate. Serve warm or cold, cut into wedges.

CHAPTER 4

MEATS

• • •

Antipasti di carne

MEAT

MEAT dishes do not play as important a role on the Italian table as they do in other cuisines, particularly the American and British. They appear as the *secondo,* "second course," of the Italian meal, preceded by the *antipasto,* if there is one, then by the *primo,* or "first course" of pasta, rice, or soup. Meat is used imaginatively with other ingredients in various courses, or it is served in small portions after a sizable carbohydrate-centered first course. ✺ Most important in the category of meat *antipasti* are *salumi,* air- and salt-cured or spiced and precooked hams, *salame,* and such. *Salumi* are prepared differently in the various regions. For example, a *prosciutto* produced in Friuli has a different flavor, texture, and look than one from Emilia or Tuscany; a *capocollo* from Calabria differs also from one produced, for example, in Apulia. Once sliced, *salumi* are called *affettati,* which essentially means "cold cuts," and they are by far the most common form of *antipasto* on the Italian table. Some sausages are eaten fresh and others are dried, which intensifies their flavor. A more thorough discussion of the various *affettati* is included in chapter 1. ✺ Probably the most prized of the *affettati* is *prosciutto crudo,* which is becoming increasingly popular in America. With its popularity, however, has come a great deal of misunderstanding about the best ways to serve and to eat it. It's a shame to do anything more to the finest *prosciutto* than to eat it raw, sliced paper-thin (although not so thin that it falls apart), accompanied perhaps only by *grissini,* Italian breadsticks (see chapter 7 for Palio's Rosemary and Sage Breadsticks). Despite the practice that persists of serving *prosciutto crudo* with figs or melon, it is best eaten on its own without sweet distractions. The tradition of eating *prosciutto* with fruit and confections came about in past times when hams were salted excessively in order to preserve them, and sweet tastes were necessary to foil the saltiness. ✺ The bone is seldom removed in Italian *prosciutti,* because it keeps the ham moist and gives it flavor. In contrast, *prosciutti* that are exported to America are boned for the convenience of being able to slice them by machine. But skillful cutting with a knife results in slices that Italian culinary expert Massimo Alberini describes as more "aggressive" and "compact" in flavor. The thickness of the slice affects the taste. Cooking this fine ham destroys its silky texture and remarkable delicacy, so it is perhaps most sensible to use the less expensive imported or domestic *prosciutti crudi* for cooking purposes. The ham should be sliced thicker when used in cooking than when eaten raw. ❀ Other common *affettati* include tongue, *bresaola, culatello, mortadella,* and *salame.* The thickness of the slice affects the flavor and texture of all *affettati.* In Italy, *mortadella* is sometimes served in finger-sized pieces on the *affettato* platter rather than round, thin slices because thicker pieces more effectively convey the subtle flavors of the fine spiced meat to the palate. ❀ Another category of meat *antipasti* are *insaccati, boudin*like sausages containing finely chopped liver, lung, and other variety meats and spices. The tasty mixtures are enclosed in a casing and either smoked or not. *Insaccati* are truly delectable and vary highly from region to region. One of the most interesting is Apulia's *salsiccia leccese,* which contains veal and pork meat flavored with lemon peel, cinnamon, and cloves. Other *insaccati* are made of veal spleen (*milza*) combined with onion, anchovies, capers, and pepper, or with livers or cockscombs. *Insaccati* are not easily made in the American kitchen, but travelers to Italy should look for them in informal restaurants and *trattorie.* ❀ A classic beginning to an elegant Italian meal is a *galantina* of capon, chicken, or veal. The meat is boned and stuffed with other ground meats, *prosciutto,* sweetbreads, pistachios or peas, and other ingredients. The whole thing is wrapped in cheesecloth and poached gently in a flavorful stock. A weight is placed on it after it is cooked, and it is served cold, in thin slices, surrounded with aspic made from the clarified stock. Clearly, this is not everyday food, but it is quintessentially Italian. *Cima alla genovese,* boned stuffed veal breast, and *vitello tonnato,* poached veal with tuna sauce, receive similar elegant treatment, and recipes for them are included in this chapter. ❀ The meat dishes that follow by no means exhaust the repertoire of meat *antipasti* dishes. Included are some of the classics, and other recipes that are probably most easily reproduced in American kitchens. ❀ ❀ ❀

INSALATA DI PETTO DI POLLO ALLA GRIGLIA

GRILLED CHICKEN BREAST SALAD

FOR 3 PEOPLE

❋

CHICKEN SALAD IS NOT TYPICALLY ITALIAN. BUT HERE IS HOW MY MOTHER ALWAYS COOKS CHICKEN BREAST FOR A SUMMER *antipasto* OR LIGHT LUNCH. THE CHICKEN BREASTS CAN ALSO BE BROILED IN THE OVEN, BUT THEY ARE ALL THE MORE TASTY IF COOKED OUTDOORS OVER CHARCOAL.

1 large whole chicken breast, boned and halved

FOR THE MARINADE:
* ❋ *2 tablespoons extra-virgin olive oil*
* ❋ *2 tablespoons freshly squeezed lemon juice*
* ❋ *¼ teaspoon salt, or to taste*
* ❋ *a little freshly milled black pepper*
* ❋ *1 clove garlic, finely chopped or passed through a garlic press*

* ❋ *½ small head escarole or chicory*
* ❋ *8 radicchio leaves*
* ❋ *1 tablespoon extra-virgin olive oil*
* ❋ *1 teaspoon freshly squeezed lemon juice*
* ❋ *additional extra-virgin olive oil and fresh lemon juice for greens*
* ❋ *½ tablespoon chopped fresh Italian parsley*
* ❋ *salt and freshly milled black pepper*

❶ PLACE EACH CHICKEN BREAST half between 2 sheets of waxed paper. Using a meat mallet or the dull side of a cleaver blade, press down and then push out from the center of each breast half, flattening it out evenly. Do not overpound or the breasts will break apart.

❷ TO MAKE THE MARINADE, combine all the ingredients in a bowl not much larger than the chicken breasts. Add the breasts, turn to coat them, cover, and marinate in the refrigerator for from 30 minutes to 2 hours. Turn the breasts occasionally.

❸ MEANWHILE, PREHEAT AN INDOOR GRILL or a broiler, or prepare hot coals in an outdoor grill. Remove the chicken breasts from the marinade, reserving the marinade, and arrange 3 to 6 inches from the heat source. Grill or broil the breasts until they are browned, turning once and brushing with marinade to keep them moist. (If there is too little marinade, brush on extra-virgin olive oil.) Plan on 3 to 4 minutes on each side; they should be cooked through but not dry.

❹ TRANSFER THE CHICKEN to a cutting board and slice the breasts on the diagonal into strips the size of a finger. Reserve the juices from the chicken. Cut the escarole or chicory and *radicchio* into manageable-sized pieces and arrange on a platter. Place the chicken strips over the greens. Pour the chicken juices, the 1 tablespoon extra-virgin olive oil, and 1 teaspoon lemon juice over the chicken. Drizzle additional oil and lemon juice on the greens, too. Strew the parsley over the chicken and then sprinkle the whole lot with salt to taste and a veil of pepper. Serve warm or at room temperature.

NOTE: Instead of serving the greens raw, the escarole, chicory, or *radicchio* can be grilled or broiled as directed on page 31 and arranged on the plate with the chicken.

INVOLTINI DI POLLO

STUFFED CHICKEN BREASTS

FOR 4 PEOPLE

A VERY PRETTY AND VERY EASY-TO-PREPARE APPETIZER. THE BONED CHICKEN BREASTS, FLATTENED, STUFFED, AND ROLLED CLOSED BEFORE COOKING, PRODUCE LITTLE CIRCLES OF CREAMY-COLORED, JUICY BREAST MEAT SURROUNDING AN HERB-SPECKLED DISK OF SAVORY STUFFING. THE PAN JUICES, WHICH ARE FORTIFIED WITH WINE, ARE POURED OVER THE FINISHED DISH AND KEEP THE CHICKEN WARM AND DELICIOUSLY MOIST.

✱ *1 large whole chicken breast, boned, skinned, and halved*

FOR THE STUFFING:
✱ *1 cup shredded coarse-textured Italian bread (crusts removed)*
✱ *½ cup chicken stock*
✱ *2 teaspoons unsalted butter*
✱ *2 or 3 green onions, white part and 1 inch of green, thinly sliced*
✱ *1 teaspoon chopped fresh sage, or ½ teaspoon dried sage*
✱ *1 teaspoon chopped fresh Italian parsley*
✱ *salt and freshly milled black pepper*
✱ *2 slices boiled ham*

✱ *1 tablespoon unsalted butter*
✱ *1 tablespoon extra-virgin olive oil*
✱ *2 heaping tablespoons all-purpose flour*
✱ *1 cup chicken stock*
✱ *¼ cup dry white wine*
✱ *chopped fresh Italian parsley for garnish*

❶ PREHEAT AN OVEN to 350 degrees F. Place each chicken breast half between 2 sheets of waxed paper. Using a meat mallet or the dull side of a cleaver blade, press down and then push out from the center of each breast half, flattening it out evenly. Do not overpound or the breasts will break apart.

❷ TO MAKE THE STUFFING, soak the bread in the stock until it is softened, 2 to 3 minutes. Meanwhile, in a skillet melt the butter over medium heat. Add the green onions and sauté until softened but not browned, about 3 minutes. Place the green onions in a mixing bowl. Squeeze the excess stock from the bread; discard the stock. Add the bread to the bowl, along with the sage, parsley, and salt and pepper to taste and mix well. Taste for seasoning.

❸ PLACE A SLICE OF HAM on each of the flattened chicken breast halves. Divide the bread stuffing between the 2 breasts, spreading it over the ham. Roll up each breast from a narrow end; the opposite end should remain uncovered and slightly overlap the roll. Tuck in any stuffing that may have leaked out of the ends; the ham slice will prevent stuffing from leaking out of the center of the chicken roll. Using cotton kitchen string, tie the rolls closed in the same fashion that a roast is laced. Toothpicks can be used to fasten the ends securely.

❹ MELT THE BUTTER with the olive oil in a skillet over medium heat. Meanwhile, dredge the chicken rolls in the flour and set aside. When the skillet is hot enough to make the chicken rolls sizzle, add them. Brown on all sides for no longer than 5 minutes. Prolonged sautéing will toughen the delicate breast meat. To turn the rolls, gently slide a spatula under them to prevent rupturing.

❺ TRANSFER THE SAUTÉED breast rolls to a casserole just large enough to accommodate them, but with enough room to keep them from touching. Set the skillet aside for later deglazing. Pour the stock over the breasts, cover tightly, and place in the preheated oven. Bake until the breasts are just cooked through but still juicy, 20 to 25 minutes. Overcooking by even 5 minutes will dry them out. Remove from the oven, and transfer the rolls to a cutting board, reserving the liquid in the casserole. Remove the string and toothpicks and let stand for 5 to 10 minutes.

❻ MEANWHILE, heat the pan drippings that remain in the skillet in which the breasts were sautéed. Add ½ cup of the stock from the casserole and bring to a simmer, using a wooden spoon to dislodge any bits stuck to the pan bottom. Add the wine and continue to simmer to evaporate the alcohol. Taste for salt.

❼ CUT EACH of the stuffed breasts crosswise into 5 or 6 slices and arrange on a serving platter. Pour the hot pan juices over them. Garnish with parsley. Serve hot or warm.

CIMA ALLA GENOVESE

STUFFED BREAST OF VEAL, GENOESE STYLE

FOR 15 TO 18 PEOPLE

❋

ima alla genovese IS A SPECIALITY OF LIGURIA, HENCE THE REFERENCE TO GENOA, LIGURIA'S CAPITAL. THE VEAL BREAST IS A VEHICLE FOR A SUCCULENT STUFFING OF GROUND MEATS, SWEETBREADS, AND SOMETIMES, SAUSAGE AND BRAIN. HARD COOKED EGGS, PEAS, AND PISTACHIO NUTS ARE ADDED TO THE STUFFING, WHICH MAKE FOR A VERY BEAUTIFUL PRESENTATION WHEN THE MEAT IS COOKED AND SLICED. I PREFER NOT TO ADD PEAS BECAUSE I DON'T LIKE TO COOK THEM FOR SO LONG, AND IN ANY CASE, THE RICH CREAMY GREEN OF THE PISTACHIOS ADDS SUFFICIENT COLOR TO THE STUFFING. ARTICHOKE HEARTS, WHEN IN SEASON, ARE A MOST AGREEABLE ADDITION TO THE STUFFING. ❋ THIS STUFFED BREAST OF VEAL IS MOST OFTEN FOUND IN *rosticcerie* AND *trattorie*, FOR DESPITE ITS ELEGANCE, IT IS CONSIDERED A FOOD OF THE PEOPLE. THE INGREDIENT LIST FOR THE RECIPE IS A LONG ONE, AND WHILE THE METHOD IS SOMEWHAT LENGTHY IN COMPARISON TO THOSE FOR MOST *antipasti*, THE DISH IS NOT A DIFFICULT ONE TO MAKE. I HAVE A PARTICULAR FONDNESS IT, FOR IT IS ONE OF THE DISHES I FIRST SERVED ON THE *Alizah*, A SAILING KETCH IN WHOSE GALLEY MY CAREER BEGAN SOME TWO DECADES AGO. I PREPARED THE DISH IN A GALLEY THE SIZE OF A KITCHEN TABLE. ❋ *Cima alla genovese* IS USUALLY SERVED COLD, BUT AS LONG AS THE VEAL HAS COOLED SUFFICIENTLY, IT CAN ALSO BE SERVED AT ROOM TEMPERATURE. THE COOKING BROTH IS DELICIOUSLY SATURATED WITH THE FLAVORS OF THE STUFFING, AND SHOULD BE STRAINED AND USED FOR AN EXTRAORDINARY SOUP. A SOUP OF THIS BROTH WITH HOME-MADE *cappelletti* OR *tortellini* WOULD BE A DISH FIT FOR THE MOST ELEGANT OCCASION. BUT EVEN THE ADDITION OF *capelli d' angelo* ("ANGEL'S HAIR") OR OTHER SOUP PASTA, WITH GRATED *parmigiano* SPRINKLED ON TOP, IS ALL THAT IS NEEDED TO TURN THE COOKING BROTH INTO A MAGNIFICENT SOUP TO FOLLOW THE *antipasto* COURSE. {*continues*}➨

FOR THE STUFFING:

* ¼ *pound sweetbreads*
* *1 tablespoon plus 1-1/4 teaspoons salt, or to taste*
* *3 ounces stale Italian or French bread*
* *milk as needed*
* ¼ *pound finely ground sweet Italian pork sausage*
* ½ *pound ground pork*
* ¼ *pound ground veal*
* *2 ounces cooked ham, chopped*
* *3 tablespoons chopped fresh Italian parsley*
* *1 tablespoon chopped fresh marjoram, or 1 teaspoon dried marjoram*
* ½ *cup freshly grated* parmigiano
* ¼ *cup pistachio nuts*
* *1 extra-large or jumbo egg, lightly beaten*
* *freshly milled black pepper*
* *2 eggs, hard-cooked and shelled*

* *half of a boned breast of veal (about 3 pounds) with pocket (see Note)*

* *2 tablespoons unsalted butter*
* *2 tablespoons olive oil*
* *1 large or 2 small carrots, peeled and quartered*
* *1 small celery stalk with leaves, cut into several pieces*
* *1 onion, quartered*
* *1 tablespoon salt*

❶ TO MAKE THE STUFFING, soak the sweetbreads in several changes of ice water for 1 hour. Drain and place in a saucepan. Add cold water to cover and the 1 tablespoon salt. Bring to a boil. Immediately lower the heat and simmer, uncovered, for 3 minutes. Meanwhile, fill a good-sized bowl with ice water. Drain the sweetbreads and immediately plunge them into the ice water until they have cooled off. Drain the sweetbreads again. Trim away all cartilage, fat, tough membranes, tubes, and dark or discolored spots. Using your hands, break up the sweetbreads into their natural small sections without tearing the fine membranes that connect them. Cover and refrigerate until chilled. Meanwhile, in a small bowl, soak the bread in milk to cover.

❷ COARSELY CHOP the sweetbreads and place in a mixing bowl. Squeeze the bread dry and add to the sweetbreads. Add the ground meats, ham, parsley, marjoram, cheese, and nuts. Mix in the beaten egg. Add the 1-¼ teaspoons salt and some pepper to taste.

❸ PUT A LITTLE of the stuffing inside the veal pocket, and place 1 of the hard-cooked eggs inside. Add more stuffing, then place the remaining hard-cooked egg in the pocket. Finally, add the remaining stuffing. Using a kitchen needle and thread, sew the veal pocket closed. Then tie the veal breast with kitchen string, much as you would tie a pot roast, so that it resembles a thick *salame*. This will facilitate lifting the *cima* in and out of the pan.

❹ SELECT A DUTCH OVEN that is large enough to hold the veal comfortably, but not excessively large. Melt the butter with the olive oil in the pan over medium heat and add the carrots and celery. Sauté until nearly golden, about 5 minutes. Add the veal, placing it in the center of the pot with the vegetables all around.

Brown it on all sides, turning it as necessary to color evenly, 15 to 20 minutes in total. When the veal is nearly browned, add the onion quarters. Sauté the onion to color lightly, then add the salt and enough water to cover the *cima*. Bring to a boil and reduce to a gentle simmer. Cover with the lid partially askew and cook for 2 hours, turning the *cima* over at the halfway point. Turn the burner off and allow the veal to cool in its own stock.

❺ LIFT THE *cima* out of the pan and place it on a platter. Place a heavy weight on top and let stand for about 2 hours; this will help to compress it into a compact shape. Remove the string and cut into thin slices. Serve at room temperature. The whole *cima* can also be refrigerated, then sliced and served cold.

NOTE: A whole veal breast with bone intact weighs approximately 9 pounds; once boned, it weighs about 6 pounds. A boned whole breast can be stuffed and served in this manner if you are planning a larger party. But as an *antipasto* for 6 to 8 people, ask the butcher to give you half the breast, and to remove the bones and cut a pocket in it (between the meat and the ribs) in which to place the stuffing. Alternatively, you can have your butcher remove the bones and "butterfly" it. Either way, you will need about 3 feet of heavy cotton kitchen string to tie the breast after it is stuffed.

AHEAD-OF-TIME NOTE: *Cima alla genovese* can be prepared up to 2 or even 3 days in advance of serving. After cooking, place the *cima* in a large bowl, cover it with its cooking stock, and refrigerate until ready to use. To serve, lift it from the bowl and slice. If the stock is utilized for soup, any leftover *cima* can be wrapped well with aluminum foil and stored in the refrigerator.

VITELLO TONNATO

POACHED VEAL WITH TUNA SAUCE

FOR 12 PEOPLE

*V*itello tonnato IS ONE OF ITALY'S GREATEST *antipasti*. ALTHOUGH IT ORIGINATED IN LOMBARDY, IT HAS BECOME POPULAR THROUGHOUT ITALY'S REGIONS. AS A RESULT, MANY VARIATIONS FOR IT HAVE COME ABOUT. WHILE THE CLASSIC *vitello tonnato* IS ALWAYS BOILED, THE MEAT CAN BE ROASTED INSTEAD. SOME VERSIONS OF THE TUNA SAUCE CONTAIN EXTRA-VIRGIN OLIVE OIL INSTEAD OF MAYONNAISE, BUT I LIKE THE CREAMY CONTRAST OF THIS SAUCE WITH THE SIMPLICITY OF THE POACHED VEAL. THE TUNA MAYONNAISE IS EQUALLY DELICIOUS ON POACHED CHICKEN, AND IS DELECTABLE SPREAD ON HALVED HARD-COOKED EGGS OR *crostini* (TOASTS, SEE PAGE 123). IT CAN ALSO BE USED AS A FILLING FOR *tramezzini* (LITTLE SANDWICHES, SEE PAGE 121). THE BEST CUT TO USE FOR *vitello tonnato* IS THE UPPER LEG, WHICH RESULTS IN TENDER, BUTTERY MEAT. VEAL SHOULDER CAN BE SUBSTITUTED, BUT IT WILL NOT PRODUCE AS REFINED A DISH AS THE LEG.

* 2 pounds meat from upper leg of veal, trimmed of fat and tied
* ¼ cup olive oil
* 1 large carrot, peeled and quartered
* 1 small celery stalk with leaves, cut into several pieces
* 1 onion, quartered
* small handful of fresh Italian parsley (stems and leaves)
* 1 cup dry white wine
* 4 cups well-flavored chicken or veal stock, or an equal amount water plus 2 teaspoons salt, or to taste

FOR THE SAUCE:
* 1 recipe Light Lemon Mayonnaise (page 127)
* 1 small can (3-½ ounces) imported Italian light tuna in olive oil, drained
* 1 tablespoon freshly squeezed lemon juice
* stock reserved from cooking veal
* 3 tablespoons drained small capers

❶ SELECT A DUTCH OVEN not much larger than the veal. Pour in the olive oil and warm over medium heat. Add the carrot, celery, onion, and parsley and brown lightly and evenly, about 5 minutes. Add the veal, placing it in the center of the pot with the vegetables all around. Brown it gently on all sides, turning as necessary to color evenly, about 25 minutes. Add the wine, pouring it over the meat as you do. Allow the alcohol to evaporate for 3 to 4 minutes. Meanwhile, bring the stock or salted water to a boil. Add it to the dutch oven and bring back to a boil. Reduce immediately to a gentle simmer. Cover and cook for 50 minutes, turning the meat frequently to bathe and cook it evenly in the stock. Turn the burner off and allow the veal to cool in the liquid.

❷ LIFT THE VEAL out of the pan and place it in a glass or ceramic bowl large enough to accommodate it and the stock. Strain the stock, discarding the vegetables, and pour it over the veal in the bowl. Cover tightly and refrigerate for 8 hours or overnight. Storing the meat in the stock will keep it moist.

❸ TO MAKE THE SAUCE, prepare the mayonnaise and place it in a bowl. Place the tuna in a food processor fitted with the metal blade and chop finely. Alternatively, chop finely by hand. Gradually beat the tuna into the mayonnaise. Blend in the lemon juice. Remove any fat that has risen to the surface of the veal stock. Add enough of the reserved stock to the mayonnaise to achieve the consistency of thin cream. Taste for salt. (Use the remaining stock for soup or some other purpose.)

❹ SPOON SOME of the tuna mayonnaise onto a large serving platter. Remove the chilled veal from the stock and cut it into very thin slices. Arrange them on the platter over the sauce, then spoon additional sauce over the veal. Sprinkle with the capers. Serve at once.

AHEAD-OF-TIME NOTE: Both the veal and the tuna sauce can be prepared up to 2 or even 3 days in advance of serving. Place the veal in a large bowl, cover with its cooking stock, and refrigerate until ready to use. The tuna sauce should also be covered and refrigerated until ready to use.

SPIEDINI DI AGNELLO CON LIMONE

SKEWERED GRILLED LAMB WITH LEMON ZEST

FOR 4 TO 6 PEOPLE

❋

THE INSPIRATION FOR THIS METHOD OF COOKING SUCCULENT LAMB MORSELS COMES FROM SARDINIA, MY MOTHER'S BIRTH-PLACE. SPIT-ROASTING MEAT IS NOT ONLY A TRADITION ON THE ISLAND OF SHEPHERDS, BUT ALSO AN ART. DROPPING THE LAMB INTO A BATH OF ICE WATER AND LEMON JUICE, THEN DRYING IT BEFORE ROASTING IN ORDER TO ENSURE A CRISP EXTE-RIOR TO THE MEAT IS A TRICK MY SARDINIAN AUNT, RITA GHISU, TAUGHT ME. I URGE YOU TO MATE THIS GRILLED LAMB WITH ARTICHOKES, A DELICIOUS COMBINATION TYPICALLY FOUND IN THE ISLAND'S CUISINE.

* *juice of 1 large lemon*
* *1 pound meat from upper leg of lamb, trimmed of fat and gristle and cut into ¾-inch dice*
* *zest of ½ lemon*
* *2 tablespoons extra-virgin olive oil*
* *1 large clove garlic, finely chopped or passed through a garlic press*
* *2 teaspoons chopped fresh rosemary, or 1 teaspoon dried rosemary*
* *coarsely milled black pepper*
* *salt*
* *fresh rosemary sprigs for garnish, if available*
* *small lemon wedges for garnish*

❶ ADD THE LEMON JUICE to a large bowl of ice water and then drop in the lamb. Soak for 10 minutes, drain, and dry the lamb thoroughly with a cotton kitchen towel.

❷ MEANWHILE, in a shallow glass or ceramic container, combine the lemon zest, olive oil, garlic, chopped or dried rosemary, and pepper to taste. Add the dried lamb cubes to the marinade, coating them well all over. Set aside at room temperature for 1 to 2 hours, turning the meat occasionally to marinate evenly.

❸ PREHEAT AN INDOOR GRILL or a broiler, or pre-pare hot coals in an outdoor grill. Thread the lamb onto thin metal skewers. Arrange the lamb skewers close to the heat source (about 6 inches in an oven broiler, about 4 inches on a grill) and broil or grill for 3 to 4 minutes on one side; turn the skewers over to finish cook-ing, 2 to 4 minutes, depending upon how well done you would like the meat. Remove from the heat and sprinkle with salt to taste. Garnish with fresh rosemary sprigs, if available, and small lemon wedges. Serve immediately.

INSALATA DI MANZO

BEEF SALAD

FOR 4 OR 5 PEOPLE

LEFTOVER MEATS HAVE MANY USES IN THE ITALIAN KITCHEN. THIS IS ONE OF THE BEST AND SIMPLEST. WITH ITS TANGY LEMON DRESSING, THIS FLAVORFUL SALAD MAKES A NICE APPETIZER, BUT IT IS ALSO A DELICIOUS AND SATISFYING LIGHT LUNCH DISH. IT IS PARTICULARLY GOOD MADE WITH LEFTOVER CHARCOAL-BROILED STEAK SUCH AS FLANK OR SKIRT STEAK, SIRLOIN, OR WHATEVER, ALTHOUGH CARE SHOULD BE TAKEN TO CUT THE MEAT INTO THIN SLICES. COLD BOILED OR ROASTED BEEF CAN ALSO BE USED.

* *1 pound grilled, roasted, or boiled beef, trimmed of fat*
* *1 tablespoon chopped fresh Italian parsley*
* *1 tablespoon drained small capers or coarsely chopped large capers*

FOR THE DRESSING:
* *1 large clove garlic, bruised*
* *½ teaspoon freshly grated lemon zest*
* *¼ cup freshly squeezed lemon juice*
* *¼ cup extra-virgin olive oil*
* *1 generous teaspoon Dijon-style mustard*
* *salt and freshly milled black pepper*

❶ CUT THE MEAT into thin, finger-sized pieces. Place it in a serving bowl with the parsley and capers.

❷ IN A SMALL BOWL, combine all the dressing ingredients, including salt and pepper to taste, and, using a fork, stir to mix. Pour the dressing over the beef and toss well. Taste for salt and pepper. Capers or any of the other seasonings can be increased according to taste.

AHEAD-OF-TIME NOTE: The dressing can be made 4 to 5 days in advance, covered, and refrigerated, then brought back to room temperature before using. Once the meat and dressing are combined, the salad can be refrigerated for several hours, or left at room temperature, covered, for 1 hour.

CROSTINI DI FEGATO ALLA TOSCANA

TOASTS WITH CHICKEN LIVER SPREAD

FOR 8 PEOPLE

❋

HERE IS A COARSE, RUSTIC PÂTÉ CLOSELY ASSOCIATED WITH TUSCAN COOKING, BUT FOUND ELSEWHERE IN ITALY AS WELL. PORK LIVERS ARE OFTEN USED FOR THIS MIXTURE, ESPECIALLY IN TUSCANY. THEY HAVE A STRONGER TASTE THAN CHICKEN LIVERS, AND MAKE AN EXCELLENT SPREAD. HAM IS USUALLY SAUTÉED WITH THE LIVERS, BUT I PREFER TO USE AMERICAN BACON, WHICH HAS AN AFFINITY WITH LIVER OF ANY KIND. THERE SHOULD NOT BE AS MANY COMPETING FLAVORS IN THIS DELICIOUS HOME-STYLE SPREAD—GARLIC, ONION, STOCK, A VARIETY OF HERBS—AS THERE ARE IN OTHER LIVER SPREADS. THE IDEA IS TO KEEP IT SIMPLE SO THAT THE CLEAR FLAVORS OF THE HARMONIOUS INGREDIENTS COME THROUGH. CHICKEN LIVERS SHOULD ALWAYS BE EXTREMELY FRESH: PLUMP, SPRINGY TO THE TOUCH, AND A DEEP BROWNISH RED. THEY MUST NEVER BE FLABBY, SPONGY, OR YELLOWISH.

❋ *4 slices lean bacon*
❋ *1 pound chicken livers*
❋ *2 tablespoons unsalted butter*
❋ *½ teaspoon salt, or to taste*
❋ *freshly milled black pepper*
❋ *1 teaspoon chopped fresh sage, or*
  ½ teaspoon dried sage
❋ *2 teaspoons brandy*
❋ *1 recipe Toasts (page 123)*
❋ *finely chopped fresh Italian parsley*
  for garnish

❶ SAUTÉ THE BACON in a skillet over medium-high heat until browned but not crisp. Remove the bacon to paper towels to blot excess fat. Chop finely and set aside. Pour the fat out of the pan.

❷ TRIM ANY FAT, connective tissue, and discolored areas from the chicken livers. Dice the livers. Place the butter in the pan that the bacon was cooked in and melt over medium-high heat. When it is bubbling hot, add the livers. Sauté, stirring to cook evenly, until cooked through but not hard, 3 to 4 minutes. Add the salt and pepper to taste. Using a slotted utensil, remove the livers to a cutting board, reserving the pan juices. Allow the livers to cool somewhat, then further chop them finely by hand.

❸ IN A BOWL combine the livers, bacon, pan juices, sage, and brandy and stir together well. Spread the liver on the *crostini.* Sprinkle with parsley and serve at room temperature.

CHAPTER 5

SEAFOOD

❖❖❖

Antipasti di mare

I REMEMBER

I REMEMBER paddling a dinghy off the beaches of my mother's native Sardinia when I was a girl, looking for sea urchins in the transparent blue-lavender of the Bay of Cagliari. Aside from diving equipment, the only things my cousins and I took with us on these forays were lemons, which we squeezed over the delicious briny flesh of the spiny creatures we caught and ate on the spot. I also remember the astonishing taste of a plate of *fritto misto di mare*, mixed fried shrimp, squid, and sole, that I had one sweltering August night twenty-five years ago in a little *trattoria* overlooking the sea near Rome. I do not remember the name of the town, and I barely remember the name of my companions. But I do remember the fish, which were so fresh, tender, and startlingly flavorful, it seemed as though the sea at the table's edge had washed right onto our plates. ❋ Many such memories of Italy's seafood are tucked away in the happy reaches of my mind, and I often call upon them when I crave a truly satisfying fish dish. It is not that Italy's fish dishes are more complex or unusual than other dishes. On the contrary, they are generally cooked more simply and with less preparation than other courses. It is the direct, fresh flavor of the sea that is so unforgettable, and that is so elusive in seafood caught outside the Mediterranean. ❋ Italian fish markets, from the most expansive near the Rialto in Venice to the small raucous ones that dot the Amalfi coast, display an amazing assortment of sea creatures. It is disappointing to find only large frozen squid in the United States when

71
FRITTO MISTO DI MARE
mixed fried seafood

72
VONGOLE AL FORNO CON PANCETTA
roasted clams with bacon

75
INSALATA DI FRUTTI DI MARE
marinated seafood salad

76
INSALATA DI BACCALÀ
salt cod salad

77
INSALATA DI RISO COI GAMBERI
shrimp and rice salad

79
GAMBERI IN PADELLA
garlicky pan-roasted shrimp

80
SCAMPI IMPANATI
breaded butterflied jumbo shrimp

80
IMPEPATA DI VONGOLE
roasted clams with extra-virgin olive oil, lemon, and parsley

81
CALAMARI ALL'INFERNO
squid "in hell"

82
SPIEDINI DI GAMBERI E CARCIOFI
skewered grilled shrimp and artichoke hearts

85
INSALATA DI ARAGOSTA CON PEPERONI ARROSTITI
lobster and roasted pepper salad

86
GAMBERETTI LESSI AL FINOCCHIO
fennel-flavored boiled small shrimp

87
SPIEDINI DI CAPESANTE
skewered grilled sea scallops

one hankers after tender, tiny ones for a *fritto misto di mare*. Or to settle for the large clams called littlenecks, cherrystones, or quahogs on the East Coast, when the best *insalata di frutti di mare* would be made with the tiny, tender, sweet orange clams one finds in Italy. Nevertheless, many excellent seafood *antipasti* can be made with what we have available to us, if only we keep them simple and use harmonious seasonings. ❋ The most common treatment of Italian seafood is a dressing of extra-virgin olive oil, lemon, and parsley. The famous *granseola* of Venice is no more than boiled crab, stripped of its shell and cartilage, tossed with this mixture. Everything from homey *baccalà,* or "salt cod," to the rich meat of lobster is enhanced by it. ❋ If ever the principle of "fresh" in cooking applies, it is here. Except for peas, even a vegetable can wait a few days before it is cooked and it will not disappoint. Not so with fish. Ideally, fish should be eaten on the same day it is caught. Otherwise, certainly no more than two days should pass between the time it is caught and cooked, and the sooner the better. ❋❋❋

FRITTO MISTO DI MARE

MIXED FRIED SEAFOOD

FOR 10 PEOPLE

THERE ARE MANY WAYS TO COOK ITALY'S FAMOUS FISH FRY—*fritto misto di mare* or *frittura di mare*. SOME ITALIANS SIMPLY DREDGE THE SEAFOOD IN FLOUR AND DEEP-FRY IT IN OLIVE OIL. OTHERS PREPARE A *pastella*, OR "BATTER," FIRST, WHICH CAN BE A SIMPLE MIXTURE OF FLOUR AND WATER, OR A MORE COMPLEX BLEND THAT ALSO CONTAINS EGGS, YEAST, WINE, OR EVEN BAKING POWDER. ❋ CERTAINLY NO BOOK ON *antipasti* WOULD BE COMPLETE WITHOUT THE INCLUSION OF RECIPES FOR BATTER-FRIED FOODS. THE ITALIANS ARE BRILLIANT AT BATTER FRYING, WHICH THEY DO WITH ALL MANNER OF VEGETABLES, FROM ARTICHOKES TO ZUC-CHINI BLOSSOMS; FRUITS, IN PARTICULAR APPLES AND BANANAS BUT ALSO STRAWBERRIES; CHEESE; CHICKEN; VARIETY MEATS; AND SEAFOOD. THE WINE IN THIS BATTER RESULTS IN A CRISPY COATING, AND SO I AM PARTICULARLY FOND OF IT. (BRANDY OR *grappa* CAN BE SUBSTITUTED FOR WHITE WINE WHEN FRYING FRUITS.) ❋ CONTRARY TO WHAT MANY PEOPLE THINK, DEEP-FRIED FOODS, IF DONE PROPERLY, ABSORB LESS OIL THAN FOODS THAT ARE SAUTÉED IN OIL OR BUTTER. IN ALL FRYING METHODS, SEVERAL RULES MUST BE HEEDED TO ENSURE THAT THE *frittura,* OR "FRIED DISH," IS CRISP AND GOLDEN. FIRST, OF COURSE, THE FISH MUST BE UNCOMPROMISINGLY FRESH. AFTER IT IS WASHED, IT MUST BE DRIED THOROUGHLY WITH PLENTY OF COTTON KITCHEN TOWELS. IT MAY SEEM EXTRAVAGANT TO USE OLIVE OIL FOR DEEP-FRYING, BUT IT GIVES A LOVELY FLAVOR TO THE SEAFOOD. USE THE BEST-QUALITY OLIVE OIL YOU CAN AFFORD (THE ITALIANS DON'T HESITATE TO USE EXTRA-VIRGIN OLIVE OIL FOR DEEP-FRYING) AND HEAT IT UNTIL IT IS QUITE HOT TO ENSURE A CRISPY CRUST. REMEMBER, YOU NEED NOT THROW THE OIL AWAY. JUST STRAIN IT THROUGH CHEESECLOTH WHEN IT COOLS, POUR IT INTO A BOTTLE, AND CAP IT. IT CAN BE USED AGAIN FOR FRYING FISH, AND THIS IS THE KIND OF DISH ONE CRAVES FROM TIME TO TIME ONCE ONE HAS EATEN IT COOKED THE CORRECT WAY.

FOR THE *pastella:*
* *1 cup less 2 tablespoons all-purpose flour*
* *½ teaspoon salt*
* *¼ teaspoon freshly milled white pepper*
* *3 tablespoons dry white wine*
* *½ cup water*
* *1-½ tablespoons olive oil*
* *1 egg, separated*

* *olive oil for deep-frying*
* *3 pounds mixed seafood, including large shrimp, peeled and deveined; squid, cleaned and cut into rings according to directions on page 81; and fish fillets such as sole, flounder, haddock, or cod*
* *2 lemons, cut into wedges*

❶ TO MAKE THE *pastella*, sift together the flour, salt, and pepper into a bowl. In a small cup stir together the wine and water and then add it to the flour mixture, mixing well. Add the oil and then the egg yolk, mixing after each addition. Cover and allow to stand at room temperature for 2 hours.

❷ BEAT THE EGG WHITE until it is thick and fold it into the batter. Pour olive oil into a deep skillet to a depth of about 2 inches. Heat to 375 degrees F, or until a bit of batter turns golden within moments of being dropped into the oil. Meanwhile, dry all the seafood thoroughly. Drop the seafood into the batter to coat even-ly, and then carefully slip it into the hot oil. Do not crowd the pan or the temperature of the oil will drop and the fish will not fry properly. If necessary, fry in batches so as not to crowd the pan. Deep-fry until golden on all sides, about 4 minutes. It is advisable to use a splat-ter shield over the pot because the squid tenta-cles cause the hot oil to splatter excessively. Remove the seafood with a slotted utensil to paper towels to drain and repeat with the remaining seafood. Sprinkle with salt to taste and serve immediately with the lemon wedges.

AHEAD-OF-TIME NOTE: The batter can be pre-pared a day in advance. After leaving it at room temperature for 2 hours, cover and refrigerate it until you are ready to use it on the following day.

VONGOLE AL FORNO CON PANCETTA

ROASTED CLAMS WITH BACON

FOR 2 PEOPLE

ITALIAN CLAMS ARE VERY SMALL—ABOUT THE SIZE OF A MAN'S THUMBNAIL—SO IT IS NOT SURPRISING THAT THIS DISH IS NEVER PRESENTED IN ITALY. ONLY LARGE CLAMS ARE SUITABLE FOR STUFFING, SO CLAMS COOKED THIS WAY ARE REALLY AN AMERICAN-ITALIAN DISH. THIS DELECTABLE APPETIZER REQUIRES EASTERN LITTLENECK CLAMS. THEY SHOULD NOT BE LARGER THAN A SILVER DOLLAR OR THEY WILL BE TOO TOUGH.

✳ *12 live littleneck clams*
✳ *salt*
✳ *cornmeal or all-purpose flour*

FOR THE TOPPING:
✳ *1 tablespoon extra-virgin olive oil*
✳ *1 small clove garlic, finely chopped or passed through a garlic press*
✳ *1 tablespoon fine dried bread crumbs*
✳ *1 tablespoon chopped roasted red sweet pepper (see Note) or bottled red sweet pepper*
✳ *1 teaspoon chopped fresh Italian parsley*
✳ *2 tablespoons finely chopped pancetta or bacon*

✳ *dry white wine for sprinkling*
✳ *1 lemon, cut into wedges*

❶ PLACE THE CLAMS in a bowl of cool water with a few big pinches of salt and a handful of cornmeal or flour. Leave in the refrigerator for at least 3 hours or overnight so that the clams will purge themselves of sand or other foreign matter. Scrub the clams to remove exterior dirt, and place them in a bowl of very hot water for 5 to 10 minutes to facilitate opening them.

❷ MEANWHILE, preheat a broiler. In a mixing bowl, combine all the ingredients for the topping and mix well.

❸ WORKING OVER A BOWL to catch any clam juice, insert a clam knife or a small, sturdy paring knife between a clam's shells and, with a horizontal movement, open the clam, thrusting the blade toward the muscle on the base of the shell. Detach the flesh from the shell cavity to make it easier to lift out when eating. Leave the whole clam meat in one of its shells and discard the other shell. Repeat with the other clams.

❹ SPOON AN EQUAL AMOUNT of the topping atop each clam. Drizzle a little of the clam juice from the bowl over the topping, then sprinkle lightly with a little wine to keep the clams moist and prevent them from burning. Place the clams in a flameproof baking dish and place the dish 9 inches from the broiler. Broil for about 6 minutes, watching carefully to be sure the topping does not burn. If it browns too quickly, move the rack farther from the flame and add a little more clam juice or wine to the top of the clams before returning them to the oven. Serve hot with lemon wedges.

NOTE: See method for roasting peppers on page 28.

INSALATA DI FRUTTI DI MARE

MARINATED SEAFOOD SALAD

FOR 6 PEOPLE

There are many different ways to make this famous antipasto, such as adding roasted red pepper. I like to keep it simple, however, so as not to distract from the clear flavor of the sea. While I list only shrimp, squid, scallops, and cockles or very small clams (West Coast steamers), other shellfish such as lobster and crab can also be used. In Italy, this salad always includes tiny cuttlefish called *seppioline*. ❋ The idea for cooking the squid with a wine cork came from Lidia Bastianich, chef and owner of Felidia in New York. She claims that the enzymes in the cork tenderize octopus during cooking. I tried it with squid and found the method successful. The most important thing for success with this recipe is, of course, that the seafood be of impeccable quality.

FOR THE COCKLES:
* 3 pounds live cockles or West Coast steamers, or 2 pounds small mussels
* salt
* cornmeal or all-purpose flour
* ¼ cup water

FOR THE SQUID:
* 1 pound squid
* 3 cups water
* 2 tablespoons red or white wine vinegar
* 1 teaspoon salt
* 2 bay leaves
* 1 wine cork

FOR THE SCALLOPS:
* 2 cups water
* 1 tablespoon red or white wine vinegar
* ½ teaspoon salt
* ½ pound bay scallops or sea scallops

FOR THE SHRIMP:
* 6 cups water
* 6 tablespoons red or white wine vinegar
* 1 tablespoon salt
* 1 pound small shrimp in the shell

FOR THE DRESSING:
* 2 large cloves garlic, bruised
* ½ cup extra-virgin olive oil
* juice of 2 lemons

* 1 tablespoon white wine vinegar
* ½ teaspoon Dijon-style mustard
* ⅛ teaspoon dried red-pepper flakes, or to taste
* ¾ teaspoon salt, or to taste
* 1 tablespoon chopped fresh Italian parsley

❶ To prepare the cockles, steamers, or mussels, place them in a bowl of cool water with a few big pinches of salt and a handful of cornmeal or flour. Leave in the refrigerator for at least 3 hours or overnight, so that the shellfish will purge themselves of sand or other foreign matter. Scrub the shells to remove exterior dirt and then rinse in cold water. If using mussels, pull off their beards. Place in a saucepan with a tightly fitting lid and add the water. Cover and cook until they open, just a few minutes. Remove from the heat immediately and drain. Remove and discard the shells, and set the meats aside in a large bowl.

❷ To prepare the squid, clean and cut as directed on page 81. In a saucepan combine the water, vinegar, salt, bay leaves, and cork. Bring to a boil, add the squid, reduce the heat to medium-low, and cook until tender, about 20 minutes. Drain and discard the bay leaves and cork. Add the squid to the bowl with the cockles.

❸ To prepare the scallops, in a saucepan combine the water, vinegar, and salt and bring to a boil. If using sea scallops, cut them in half or in quarters, depending upon their size. Add the scallops to the boiling water and boil for 3 minutes. Drain and add to the bowl with the other seafood.

❹ To prepare the shrimp, in a saucepan combine the water, vinegar, and salt. Bring to a boil, add the shrimp, and boil for 3 minutes. Drain and when cool enough to handle, remove the peels and the dark intestinal vein. Add the shrimp to the bowl with the other seafood.

❺ In a small bowl, whisk together all the dressing ingredients. Taste and adjust the seasonings. Pour the dressing over the seafood and toss well. Cover and marinate at room temperature for 1 to 2 hours before serving.

NOTE: This dish is best served no more than 5 hours after it is prepared. It should marinate at room temperature; the flavors of the seafood are arrested under refrigeration. If it is necessary to chill the salad, cover it tightly with plastic wrap and refrigerate for up to 24 hours. Allow it to return to room temperature before serving.

INSALATA DI BACCALÀ

SALT COD SALAD

FOR 4 TO 6 PEOPLE

THE ITALIANS, NORTHERNERS AND SOUTHERNERS ALIKE, ARE FOND OF *baccalà*, OR "SALT COD." NUMEROUS TASTY RECIPES FOR *baccalà* HAVE COME ABOUT AS A RESULT OF ITS PROLIFIC USE DURING CHRISTIAN DAYS OF ABSTINENCE, WHEN MEAT-EATING WAS TRADITIONALLY FORBIDDEN. MANY AMERICANS ARE LIKELY TO WONDER WHAT COULD POSSIBLY BE APPEALING ABOUT THESE EMACIATED SLABS OF DRIED, SALTED FISH. BUT ONCE REVIVED AFTER SOAKING AND COOKING, *baccalà* IS ENORMOUSLY TASTY AND VERSATILE. IT IS IMPORTANT, HOWEVER, TO SELECT THE SKINLESS AND BONELESS VARIETY, WHICH ELIMINATES TEDIOUS AND UNNECESSARY PREPARATION. LOOK FOR MEATY, CREAMY-COLORED FILLETS; AVOID EXCESSIVELY THIN, BROWN PIECES. THIS DRESSING CAN ALSO BE USED FOR SALADS MADE FROM FRESH FISH FILLETS OR FOR BOILED CRAB MEAT.

✱ *1-½ pounds skinless, boneless* baccalà
✱ *thick apple slice or 1/2 potato*
✱ *3 tablespoons extra-virgin olive oil*
✱ *1-½ tablespoons freshly squeezed lemon juice*
✱ *1 small clove garlic, finely chopped*
✱ *freshly milled black pepper*
✱ *1 tablespoon chopped fresh Italian parsley*

❶ TO PREPARE THE SALT COD, place it in a bowl and add cold water to cover and the apple or potato, which helps to draw out the salt. Refrigerate overnight, changing the water several times during the soaking. Drain the salt cod and rinse in fresh cool water.

❷ PLACE THE COD in a pan with cold water to cover. Bring to a boil, then reduce the heat and cook gently until the fish is tender but not falling apart, 15 to 20 minutes. Taste it before draining to make sure it is cooked. If it is still too hard, continue cooking it gently. If you find it still too salty at this point, cover with fresh cold water, bring to a boil again, and drain and rinse. When the fish is tender, drain and rinse under cold water. Drain well and pat dry with a cotton kitchen towel. Check for any skin and bones that may have been missed.

❸ Break up the fish into large flakes and transfer to a serving plate. In a small bowl stir together the oil, lemon juice, garlic, and pepper to taste. Drizzle over the fish. Sprinkle with the parsley. Serve at room temperature.

INSALATA DI RISO COI GAMBERI

SHRIMP AND RICE SALAD

FOR 10 TO 12 PEOPLE

❋

WHILE PASTA SALADS ARE HERETICAL TO GOOD ITALIAN COOKING, RICE SALADS ARE TYPICAL. EVEN WHEN MARINATED IN ACIDIC DRESSINGS, RICE RETAINS ITS FIRM TEXTURE. RICE SALADS MIGHT INCLUDE CHICKEN, LOBSTER, SMOKED SAUSAGES, TUNA, OLIVES, OR CAPERS, AMONG OTHER THINGS. THIS LEMONY RICE AND SHRIMP SALAD IS A FAVORITE OF MINE. ACTUALLY, THERE SHOULD BE MORE SHRIMP THAN RICE, BUT ABOVE ALL, DO NOT OVERCOOK THE RICE. THE KERNELS SHOULD EASILY SEPARATE FROM EACH OTHER WHEN LIFTED WITH A FORK. RINSING THE RICE AFTER COOKING PREVENTS THE GRAINS FROM STICKING TOGETHER.

FOR THE STOCK:
* *1 large carrot, peeled and cut crosswise into eighths*
* *several fresh Italian parsley sprigs, with stems intact*
* *1 small onion, cut in half*
* *3 tablespoons red wine vinegar*

* *salt as needed*
* *2-½ pounds small shrimp, peeled, deveined, and split in half lengthwise*
* *1 cup long-grain white rice*
* *5 tablespoons extra-virgin olive oil, or to taste*
* *juice of 1 large lemon*
* *⅓ pound sugar snap peas or fresh or frozen shelled green peas, blanched for 1 minute and drained*
* *½ cup* pinoli *(pine nuts), lightly toasted*
* *¼ pound cooked ham, diced*
* *4 green onions, including some green tops, thinly sliced*
* *3 tablespoons chopped fresh Italian parsley*
* *⅛ teaspoon freshly grated nutmeg, or to taste*
* *freshly milled black pepper*

❶ TO MAKE THE STOCK, in a saucepan combine the carrot, parsley, onion, and vinegar with enough cold water to cover the shrimp eventually. Bring to a boil and simmer for 15 minutes. Add 2 teaspoons salt and the shrimp, cover, and cook over high heat just until the shrimp turns pink, about 1-½ minutes. Do not overcook them or they will harden. Drain immediately and set aside.

❷ MEANWHILE, bring plenty of water to a boil and add the rice and 1 tablespoon salt. Reduce the heat to low and cook until tender but firm to the bite, about 12 minutes. Drain immediately and rinse in cold water. Drain well again and place in a serving bowl. Add the oil to the rice when it is still somewhat warm and toss lightly. The warmth of the rice will bring out the flavor of the extra-virgin olive oil. Add the lemon juice, toss again, and then add all the remaining ingredients, including salt and pepper to taste. Serve at room temperature.

AHEAD-OF-TIME NOTE: The salad can be made 3 hours in advance. It is best if it is not refrigerated before serving. The lemon juice should be added at the last minute if the salad is assembled ahead of time.

GAMBERI IN PADELLA

GARLICKY PAN-ROASTED SHRIMP

FOR 4 PEOPLE

HERE IS ONE OF THE MOST POPULAR WAYS FOR COOKING SHRIMP IN ITALY AND THROUGHOUT THE MEDITERRANEAN. IN AMERICAN-ITALIAN CUISINE, THIS RECIPE WOULD BE REFERRED TO AS "SHRIMP SCAMPI," A CURIOUS TITLE SINCE *scampi* MEANS SHRIMP, WHICH MEANS THE NAME, LITERALLY TRANSLATED, IS "SHRIMP SHRIMP." GOOD ITALIAN OR FRENCH BREAD SHOULD ALWAYS BE SERVED WITH THIS DISH FOR SOPPING UP THE GOOD GARLICKY SAUCE.

- *1/2 pound large shrimp, peeled*
- *2 teaspoons sea salt*
- *1/4 cup extra-virgin olive oil*
- *2 large cloves garlic, finely chopped or passed through a garlic press*
- *pinch of dried red-pepper flakes, or 1 or 2 whole dried* peperoncini *(hot peppers)*
- *1/4 teaspoon salt, or to taste*
- *2 tablespoons dry white wine*
- *1 tablespoon chopped fresh Italian parsley*

❶ REMOVE THE DARK intestinal veins from the shrimp. As you do, make each cut deep enough to butterfly the shrimp, so each can be opened flat like a book. Fill a bowl with ice water, add the sea salt and the butterflied shrimp, and let stand for 15 minutes to bring out some of the briny flavor of the shellfish. (Removing their shells robs the shrimp of some of their natural flavor.) Drain and dry thoroughly with a cotton kitchen towel.

❷ IN A LARGE SKILLET over medium heat, warm the olive oil. Add the garlic and hot pepper and sauté gently until the garlic softens but is not browned, about 2 minutes. Add the shrimp, placing them opened flat on the bottom of the pan so they do not curl too much. Sauté, turning once, until they are opaque, about 2 minutes on each side. Add the wine, stir and cook for an additional 30 seconds to allow alcohol to evaporate. Remove and discard the whole peppers, if using. Sprinkle with parsley and serve immediately.

VARIATION WITH TOMATO: Add 1 small ripe tomato, peeled, seeded, and coarsely chopped, or 2 canned plum tomatoes, seeded and coarsely chopped, to the sautéed shrimp in the skillet. Stir to mix, then add the wine and proceed with the recipe.

SCAMPI IMPANATI

BREADED BUTTERFLIED JUMBO SHRIMP

FOR 2 PEOPLE

❁

I LOVE THIS CLASSIC ITALIAN WAY OF COOKING SHRIMP. IT IS VERY QUICK AND ACHIEVES SOME OF THE SAME TASTY RESULTS OF DEEP-FRYING WITHOUT FRYING AT ALL. THE CRUMB MIXTURE FORMS A SLIGHTLY CRUNCHY, MILDLY GARLICKY COATING AND SEALS IN THE NATURAL JUICES OF THE SHELLFISH.

* *½ pound jumbo shrimp, peeled*

FOR THE COATING:
* *3 tablespoons fine dried bread crumbs*
* *1 tablespoon chopped fresh Italian parsley*
* *1 clove garlic, finely chopped or passed through a garlic press*
* *2 tablespoons extra-virgin olive oil*
* *scant ¼ teaspoon salt*
* *freshly milled black pepper*

* *olive oil for oiling baking pan*
* *1 small lemon, cut into wedges (optional)*

❶ PREHEAT AN OVEN to 400 degrees F. Meanwhile, thoroughly dry the shrimp and then remove the dark intestinal vein from each one. As you do, make each cut deep enough to butterfly the shrimp, so each can be opened flat like a book.

❷ COMBINE ALL THE ingredients for the coating, including pepper to taste. Oil a shallow baking pan large enough to hold the shrimp without crowding. Press each shrimp into the coating mixture, covering it well on both sides. (Do not do this until just before you are ready to bake the shrimp, or the coating will get soggy.) Place the shrimp in the baking pan without allowing them to touch each other. Place the pan on the upper rack of the preheated oven and cook until the crust is golden and the shrimp are cooked through but not dried out, 6 to 7 minutes.

❸ THESE SHRIMP ARE best straight out of the oven, piping hot. Serve with lemon wedges, if you like.

IMPEPATA DI VONGOLE

ROASTED CLAMS WITH EXTRA-VIRGIN OLIVE OIL, LEMON, AND PARSLEY

FOR 4 PEOPLE

❁

FROM CAMPANIA, HERE IS A SIMPLE METHOD FOR COOKING CLAMS OR MUSSELS. THE CLAMS ARE ROASTED, ALTHOUGH THEY COULD ALSO BE STEAMED, AND THEN ANOINTED WITH A GENEROUS SPLASH OF FRUITY OLIVE OIL AND LEMON JUICE AND A SCATTERING OF FRESH PARSLEY. THE SHELLFISH MUST BE IMPECCABLY FRESH, OF COURSE, AND ALSO SMALL AND TENDER, AND THEY SHOULD BE SERVED PIPING HOT. THE SMALL, SWEET STEAMER CLAMS OF THE PACIFIC NORTHWEST CALLED FOR IN THIS RECIPE ARE NOT TO BE CONFUSED WITH EAST COAST STEAMERS, WHICH ARE A TOTALLY DIFFERENT MOLLUSK.

* *24 live littleneck clams, or 2 pounds*
  West Coast steamer clams or small tender mussels
* *salt*
* *cornmeal or all-purpose flour*
* *2 tablespoons water, boiling*
* *extra-virgin olive oil for drizzling*
* *plenty of freshly milled black pepper*
* *3 tablespoons chopped fresh Italian parsley*
* *1 lemon, cut into wedges*

❶ PLACE THE CLAMS OR MUSSELS in a bowl of cool water with a few big pinches of salt and a handful of cornmeal or flour. Leave in the refrigerator for at least 3 hours or overnight so that the clams or mussels will purge themselves of sand or other foreign matter. Scrub the shells to remove exterior dirt and then rinse in cold water. If using mussels, pull off their beards.

❷ MEANWHILE, preheat an oven to 450 degrees F. Arrange the shellfish in an ovenproof dish. Add the boiling water to the bottom of the dish and slide the dish onto the top rack of the oven. The shellfish will open in 12 to 15 minutes.

❸ WHEN ALL OF THEM HAVE OPENED, remove from the oven. Drain off excess juice so as not to dilute the olive oil too much. Place the shellfish in individual serving bowls and drizzle the meat of each generously with oil. Then sprinkle with pepper to taste and the parsley. Serve with lemon wedges.

CALAMARI ALL'INFERNO

SQUID "IN HELL"

FOR 2 TO 3 PEOPLE

✤

THIS IS A VARIATION ON A GENOESE *antipasto* THAT IS MADE WITH TINY OCTOPUS CALLED *moscardine*. SQUID—THE SMALLEST AVAILABLE—ARE A GOOD SUBSTITUTE. THE FISH ARE ESSENTIALLY STEWED IN A HOT, HEADY TOMATO-BASED SAUCE THAT MAY INCLUDE RED WINE. I LIKE TO USE WINE VINEGAR, WHICH GIVES THE DISH A LOVELY TANGINESS THAT IS APPROPRIATE FOR AN APPETIZER COURSE. SERVE WITH PLENTY OF GOOD CRUSTY ITALIAN BREAD SO THAT THE DELICIOUS SAUCE DOES NOT GO TO WASTE.

✳ *1-½ pounds small squid*
✳ *1 pound ripe plum tomatoes or other vine-ripened tomatoes, or 1 cup canned plum tomatoes, drained, seeded, and chopped*
✳ *3 tablespoons extra-virgin olive oil*
✳ *2 large cloves garlic, grated or chopped*
✳ *1 tablespoon tomato paste*
✳ *1 teaspoon chopped fresh rosemary, or ½ teaspoon dried rosemary*
✳ *1 teaspoon salt, or to taste*
✳ *⅛ teaspoon dried red-pepper flakes, or to taste*
✳ *1 tablespoon red or white wine vinegar*
✳ *1 tablespoon chopped fresh Italian parsley*

❶ TO CLEAN THE SQUID, separate the head and tentacles from the body by grasping the head below the eyes and pulling this top section from the body cavity in a smooth motion. Remove and discard the ink sac from the head. Place the squid body in a bowl of water, or hold it under running cold water, and peel off the speckled skin. Remove the cellophane-like "spine" from the body and clean out any insides remaining in the cavity. Rinse the body thoroughly to remove all traces of ink. Cut the head from the tentacles at the "waist," above the eyes, and remove the hard "beak" from the base of the tentacles. Cut the body into rings ¼ inch wide. Cut the tentacles into halves or quarters, depending upon their size. Rinse and dry the squid pieces thoroughly.

❷ IF USING FRESH TOMATOES, bring a saucepan filled with water to a boil, add the tomatoes, and blanch for 30 seconds. Remove from the water and, when cool enough to handle, peel them and cut in half crosswise. Remove and discard their seeds, and then cut into medium dice. You will have about 1 cup; set aside.

❸ IN A SKILLET over medium heat, warm the oil and garlic. Sauté the garlic until it softens, about 2 minutes. Add the squid and sauté for 3 to 4 minutes. Add the tomato paste, tomatoes, rosemary, salt, pepper flakes, and vinegar. Simmer over gentle heat, partially covered, until the squid are tender, about 25 minutes. Stir in the parsley. Serve in bowls.

SPIEDINI DI GAMBERI E CARCIOFI

SKEWERED GRILLED SHRIMP AND ARTICHOKE HEARTS

FOR 4 PEOPLE

❋

THESE TASTY SHRIMP CAN BE GRILLED OR BROILED WITH OR WITHOUT THEIR SHELLS, ALTHOUGH LEAVING THEIR SHELLS INTACT SEALS IN THEIR NATURAL OCEAN FLAVOR. ARTICHOKES ARE USUALLY ASSOCIATED WITH EARTH FOODS, NOT SEAFOODS. BUT THE SMOKINESS OF THE GRILL BRINGS THE TWO FLAVORS TOGETHER IN A LOVELY WAY. IF YOU FAIL TO FIND TENDER, FRESH ARTICHOKES, SIMPLY GRILL THE SHRIMP BY THEMSELVES.

* *2 teaspoons sea salt*
* *½ pound medium-sized or large shrimp*
* *2 artichokes (about ½ pound each)*
* *2 medium-sized plus 1 large clove garlic*
* *1 bay leaf*
* *1 small onion, cut lengthwise into quarters*
* *3 tablespoons extra-virgin olive oil*
* *freshly milled black pepper*
* *salt*

❶ FILL A BOWL with ice water and add the sea salt. Whether keeping the shells on the shrimp or removing them, make a cut right down their backs and remove the dark intestinal vein. You can do this with the shells on by cutting through the shells. As the shrimp are prepared, drop them into the ice water. Let stand for 15 to 30 minutes. Drain and dry well with a cotton kitchen towel. Meanwhile, trim the artichokes as directed on page 53, but leave whole.

❷ IN A SAUCEPAN pour in enough water to cover the artichokes. Slice the 2 medium-sized garlic cloves and add them to the water, along with the bay leaf and onion. Bring to a boil and drop in the artichokes. Cook until tender but still firm (cooking time will depend upon how fresh they are). Drain and cut lengthwise into eighths.

❸ FINELY CHOP the remaining large garlic clove and place in a mixing bowl or pass it through a garlic press into the bowl. Add the olive oil, pepper to taste, and the shrimp. Using your hands, massage the marinade into the shrimp. Cover tightly and place in the refrigerator for at least 30 minutes, or for up to several hours.

❹ PREPARE A FIRE in a charcoal grill or preheat an indoor grill or a broiler. Position the rack close to the heat source. Alternate the artichoke pieces with the shrimp on metal skewers, passing the skewers straight through the middle of the shrimp to straighten them so that they will cook evenly. Brush the artichokes with any of the marinade that remains from the shrimp.

❺ PLACE THE SKEWERS on the grill or in a pan in the broiler and grill or broil shrimp in the shell for 2 minutes on the first side and 1-½ minutes on the second side. Shelled shrimp should be grilled or broiled for 1-½ minutes on the first side and 1 minute on the second. The outside of each shrimp should be crispy and charred, while the inside should be moist and tender. The artichokes will take on a lovely brinish flavor from the shellfish. Sprinkle to taste with salt and eat immediately.

INSALATA DI ARAGOSTA CON PEPERONI ARROSTITI

LOBSTER AND ROASTED PEPPER SALAD

FOR 3 OR 4 PEOPLE

❋

T HE SWEET RICHNESS OF THE LOBSTER AND THE PUNGENT, SMOKY FLAVOR OF THE PEPPERS, SO VIBRANTLY AND DEEPLY COLORED IN CONTRAST TO THE CREAMY WHITE, PINK-TINGED LOBSTER MEAT MAKE AN ASTONISHINGLY GOOD COMBINATION. THERE IS NO NEED FOR SALT, GARLIC, OR ONION. THE NATURAL INTENSITY OF BOTH THE LOBSTER AND THE PEPPERS IS MORE THAN SUFFICIENT; ANOTHER BOLD ELEMENT WOULD ONLY BE AN INTRUSION. BUT A TOUCH OF SWEET FRESH BASIL MARRIES THE FLAVORS IN A LOVELY WAY.

* *1 yellow bell pepper*
* *1 red bell pepper*
* *2 live lobsters (1-¼ to 1-½ pounds each)*
* *extra-virgin olive oil*
* *1 teaspoon freshly squeezed lemon juice*
* *12 fresh basil leaves, torn into pieces*

❶ ROAST THE PEPPERS, then peel and seed them as directed on page 27. Cut them into strips about ½ inch wide and 2 inches long and set aside.

❷ WHILE THE PEPPERS are roasting, pour water to a depth of 1 inch in the bottom of a steamer pan with a tight-fitting lid and bring to a boil. Place the live lobsters in the steamer insert and cover the steamer. Close any vent holes on the lid. Cook over medium heat until the lobsters turn bright red, 12 to 15 minutes.

❸ REMOVE THE LOBSTERS from the pot and, when they are cool enough to handle, remove the tail and claw meat from the shells. Remove the intestinal vein that runs down the center of each tail. Cut the lobster meat into bite-sized pieces.

❹ IN AN ATTRACTIVE serving bowl, combine the lobster meat with the pepper strips. Drizzle with olive oil to taste and then the lemon juice. Sprinkle with the basil. Serve warm or at room temperature.

AHEAD-OF-TIME NOTE: This dish can be assembled up to 8 hours in advance, covered, and refrigerated. The peppers can be roasted, cleaned, and cut 3 to 4 days in advance. Bring the dish to room temperature before serving.

GAMBERETTI LESSI AL FINOCCHIO

FENNEL-FLAVORED BOILED SMALL SHRIMP

FOR 4 PEOPLE

IT CAN BE TEDIOUS TO REMOVE SHELLS FROM SHRIMP AFTER COOKING BECAUSE THEY DO NOT SLIP OFF AS EASILY, BUT THE SHELL-FISH WILL HAVE BETTER FLAVOR. THE FENNEL IN THE COOKING WATER ADDS A DELIGHTFUL SWEETNESS TO THE SHRIMP. THERE IS NO NEED FOR ANY CONTRASTING FLAVOR SUCH AS LEMON OR VINEGAR, WHICH WOULD JUST MASK AND MUDDLE THE NATURAL ANISEY NOTES OF THE FENNEL. SERVE RAW FENNEL WITH THE COOKED SHRIMP TO BRING OUT THIS FLAVOR EVEN FURTHER, AND FOR A LOVELY CONTRAST IN TEXTURES.

* *1 large fennel bulb with stalks and leaves intact*
* *1 small carrot, peeled and quartered*
* *2 tablespoons white or red wine vinegar*
* *½ teaspoon whole black peppercorns*
* *2 teaspoons sea salt*
* *1 pound small shrimp in the shell*
* *3 tablespoons extra-virgin olive oil*

❶ CUT 1 LARGE stalk with leaves from the fennel bulb. Cut the stalk into thirds and place in a saucepan large enough to hold the shrimp eventually. Add the carrot, vinegar, peppercorns, and plenty of cold water to cover the shrimp eventually. Bring to a boil and simmer for 5 minutes to create a light stock.

❷ MEANWHILE, trim off any brown or discolored spots from the fennel bulb. Cut a thick slice off the bottom of the fennel bulb in order to separate the stalks easily. Cut off the tough, dark green upper part of the stalks (save them for flavoring stocks or soups). Keep the trimmed fennel on ice or refrigerated in a plastic bag until the shrimp are cooked and cleaned.

❸ ADD THE SALT and the shrimp to the boiling stock. Cover the pot and cook over high heat until the shrimp are opaque. Small shrimp cook quickly, in about 2 minutes from the second they are dropped into the boiling water. It is important they not overcook, or they will lose their delicate flavor and texture. Drain and, when cool enough to handle, remove the shells and every bit of the dark intestinal vein. Place in a bowl and toss with the oil. Arrange on a serving platter along with the chilled fennel. Serve warm or at room temperature.

SPIEDINI DI CAPESANTE

SKEWERED GRILLED SEA SCALLOPS

FOR 4 PEOPLE

❋

OUTHERN ITALIANS DO NOT TRADITIONALLY PREPARE SCALLOPS BECAUSE THEY ARE NOT INDIGENOUS TO MEDITERRANEAN WATERS. THEY ARE NATIVE TO THE ADRIATIC, AND ARE MOST TYPICALLY FOUND IN THE COOKING OF THE VENETO AND OF EMILIA-ROMAGNA. GRILLING, PARTICULARLY OVER WOOD OR CHARCOAL, IS A COMMON WAY OF COOKING THESE SWEET SHELL-FISH. ALTHOUGH LEMON JUICE IS OFTEN USED IN MARINADES FOR SCALLOPS AND OTHER SEAFOOD, IT, AS WELL AS OTHER LIQ-UIDS, PREVENTS THE SEAFOOD FROM SEARING PROPERLY. INSTEAD, I USE LEMON ZEST, WHICH GIVES A TANGY LEMON FLAVOR AND ALLOWS FISH AND SHELLFISH TO COLOR NICELY ON THE OUTSIDE WHILE STILL LOCKING IN FLAVORS. THE PUNCH OF THE LEMON ZEST MAKES SALT UNNECESSARY, BUT YOU CAN ADD IT IF YOU LIKE ONCE THE SCALLOPS ARE COOKED. WHETHER GRILLING OVER CHARCOAL OR UNDER A BROILER, BE SURE THE SCALLOPS ARE VERY CLOSE TO THE FLAME SO THEY ARE SEARED ON THE OUTSIDE BUT NOT OVER-COOKED WITHIN.

FOR THE MARINADE:
- *1/2 small clove garlic, finely chopped or passed through a garlic press*
- *2 teaspoons extra-virgin olive oil*
- *½ teaspoon freshly grated lemon zest*
- *2 fresh basil leaves, chopped*
- *freshly milled black pepper*

- *16 sea scallops (about ½ pound), dried thoroughly*
- *salt to taste (optional)*

❶ IN A SHALLOW BOWL, stir together all the ingredients for the marinade, including pepper to taste. Add the scallops, and stir with a wooden spoon to coat well. Cover and refrigerate for 30 minutes to 1 hour. Turn the scallops in the marinade occasionally (or at least once) to marinate evenly.

❷ MEANWHILE, prepare a fire in a charcoal grill or preheat an indoor grill or a broiler. Divide the scallops evenly among 4 metal skewers. Grill or broil, turning once, until tender, 2 minutes on each side. Sprinkle with salt, if you like (but taste first). Serve hot.

AHEAD-OF-TIME NOTE: The scallops can be left in the marinade, refrigerated, for up to 12 hours before cooking.

CHAPTER 6

POLENTA & BEANS

∗∗∗

Antipasti di polenta e fagioli

POLENTA

POLENTA originates in the ancient *puls* (or plural, *pultes*) of the Etruscans and the Romans, a pasty porridge of lentils, beans, millet, or barley. Soon after Christopher Columbus brought a pocketful of corn kernels back to Italy with him from the New World, the grain, dubbed *grano turco,* was cultivated in Italy and made into flour for *polenta,* cornmeal mush. *Polenta* eventually took its firmest hold in Lombardy, Piedmont, and the Veneto, and for four hundred years it has been a basic staple in these mountainous regions where food was simple and sometimes scarce. Today, however, this dish carries no class distinction. Its preparation can be rustic or refined, and its uses are as varied as the rich imaginations of Italy's cooks. ❋ *Polenta* is made of white or yellow corn. In Liguria, the Valtellina, and other Alpine regions, it is made from buckwheat *(polenta taragna)* as well. The corn can be either coarsely or finely ground cornmeal, and in Italy both types are used. Fine cornmeal is often used when a looser *polenta* is desired for serving with a *ragù* or other rich sauce. The coarse meal produces a grittier, more rustic *polenta,* that the Italians say can be sensed *sotto i denti,* literally, "under the teeth." The coarser meal usually has more corn flavor, and I recommend it for all the recipes included here. Among the possibilities for *polenta*-based *antipasti* are croquettes, *sformati* ("molds"), *crostini* (fried or grilled toasts) served plain or topped with anything from smoked salmon to creamed salt cod (called *baccalà mantecato*), and miniature *polenta*-square sandwiches, which might be filled with *prosciutto, gorgonzola,* or the chicken liver pâté on page 67. ❋ As for beans, they were an ancient food of the *cucina povera,* or "poor kitchen," as the Italians fondly call their essentially peasant-based cuisine. Pellegrino Artusi, in his 1895 culinary bible, *La scienza in cucina e l'arte di mangiar bene,* called them "the meat of the poor." But the Italian housewife, rich or poor, looked to heaven as well as to the purse when contemplating what to put on the dinner table. On Fridays, the Catholic religion forbade consumption of animal flesh; therefore, a meatless menu had to be devised. Thus a host of bean dishes evolved based on local customs, geography, and resources. ❋ The Tuscans, dubbed *mangiafagioli*—"bean eaters"—by their country-men, are perhaps most famous for their bean dishes, which are uncomplicated and direct. In the quintessential Tuscan dish, *fagioli al fiasco,* the beans are cooked in a flask with nothing else so that all of their flavor is sealed in. The flask is buried under the ashes and coals of the fireplace to cook the beans slowly until they are tender. Nothing more than fruity extra-virgin olive oil, salt, and pepper is added. Another signature dish of the Tuscans is *fagioli all'uccelletto,* literally, "beans like birds," named, according to Waverley Root in *The Food of Italy,* because their flavoring of tomato, sage, and garlic makes them taste like game birds. ❀ While the Tuscans prefer white beans, the northerners rely on creamy-colored magenta-speckled *borlotti,* a relation of the cranberry bean. Favas (broad beans) and chick-peas find favor in Lazio, Apulia, Sicily, and many other southern regions, although they are found throughout Italy. Beans and lentils (not actually beans by a botanist's definition) have many uses in the Italian kitchen. On the *antipasto* table these include the Apulian *'ncapriata,* a dish of puréed dried fava beans flavored with garlic, rich Apulian olive oil, and black pepper, reminiscent of *hummus;* bean salads in which anything from tinned tuna to diced salted beef might appear; and tender *cannellini* beans and small shrimp flavored with tomato, basil, and garlic, a specialty of Tuscany. Raw young fava beans eaten with sharp local *pecorino romano* is a passion of the Romans in springtime, while in Tuscany, they are combined with local *pecorino, prosciutto,* pepper, and thick olive oil in a salad. In Sicily, fava beans are stewed with garlic and mint; in Sardinia, with garlic and parsley. In other parts of Italy, fava beans are simmered gently in extra-virgin olive oil with flecks of *prosciutto* and finely sliced spring onions. ❀ It is rare to find fresh shell beans in America, and so I have refrained from giving recipes for fava beans, even though they are among my favorite foods. There are, however, numerous varieties of dried beans available to us. Chapter 1 carries information on soaking and cooking them, as well as tips on using canned beans. ❀ ❀ ❀

POLENTA

BASIC POLENTA

FOR 6 PEOPLE

Polenta APPEARS ON THE ITALIAN TABLE IN MANY FORMS. IN ITS SIMPLEST GUISE IT IS SERVED "LOOSE," AS A SORT OF PORRIDGE WITH BUTTER AND GRATED *parmigiano*. FOR A MORE COMPLEX DISH, IT IS TURNED OUT ONTO A MARBLE SLAB OR OTHER HARD SURFACE, ALLOWED TO HARDEN, AND THEN CUT INTO PIECES. THESE PIECES HAVE ENDLESS USES, ESPECIALLY FOR *antipasti*. WHEN FRIED IN OLIVE OIL, SAUTÉED IN BUTTER, OR BRUSHED WITH BUTTER AND GRILLED, THEY BECOME *crostini di polenta,* DELICIOUS CRUNCHY "TOASTS." ❋ ALTHOUGH *polenta* IS AS SIMPLE TO COOK AS A BOILED EGG, THERE IS A CERTAIN MYSTIQUE ASSOCIATED WITH ITS PREPARATION. TRADITIONALLY, A SPECIAL COPPER POT AND HEAVY WOODEN SPOON WERE RESERVED FOR MAKING IT. A WOMAN WHO EMIGRATED FROM TRIESTE TO THE UNITED STATES TOLD ME THAT THE ONLY POSSESSIONS SHE BROUGHT WITH HER BESIDES HER CLOTHING WERE HER COPPER *paiolo* AND WOODEN *bastone,* THE TRADITIONAL IMPLEMENTS THAT HAVE BEEN USED FOR CENTURIES FOR MAKING *polenta* IN THE NORTHERN REGIONS. ANY GOOD QUALITY, HEAVY-BOTTOMED POT WILL DO, HOWEVER. IT IS HELPFUL TO USE A WOODEN SPOON WITH A LONG HANDLE FOR STIRRING, BECAUSE ONCE THE *polenta* BUBBLES, IT CAN SPLATTER YOUR HAND. THE WHISK IS NOT COMMONLY USED IN ITALY, AND IS EVEN CONSIDERED BY SOME TO BE HERETICAL. BUT I HAVE FOUND THAT A GOOD, STRONG, HEAVY WHISK TURNS OUT A FINE, LUMP-FREE *polenta.* ❋ THE REAL SECRET IS NOT SO MUCH IN THE INSTRUMENTS AS IN THE METHODOLOGY: FOR PERFECT *polenta,* DEVOTED, NONSTOP, ENERGETIC STIRRING IS ESSENTIAL. CONSTANT STIRRING, ALONG WITH THE SLOW, REGULAR ADDITION OF THE CORNMEAL, ASSURES THAT IT IS INCORPORATED WITHOUT LUMPS. ALWAYS STIR IN THE SAME DIRECTION TO KEEP THE TEXTURE SMOOTH AND UNIFORM. IF IT SEEMS TO BE GETTING HARD BEFORE IT IS COOKED, ADD BOILING WATER, A LITTLE AT A TIME, TO KEEP IT SOFT AND EASY TO STIR. IT IS READY WHEN IT CAN EASILY BE PULLED AWAY FROM THE SIDES OF THE PAN WITH A SPOON.

7 cups water
1 tablespoon salt
2 cups coarse cornmeal
boiling water as needed

❶ BRING THE WATER to a boil in a deep pot. Add the salt. Then add the cornmeal very slowly, almost in a trickle (*a doccia,* "like a shower"). Adding the cornmeal gradually is important, for it will prevent lumps from forming and keep the boiling temperature constant, which is important if the *polenta* is to be soft and creamy. The flame should be set at medium heat so that the *polenta* continues to boil. If the heat is too low, it will simply stew and not cook properly. From the instant the cornmeal is added to the water, continuously stir it with a long-handled wooden spoon, always in the same direction. After all the cornmeal is absorbed, continue to stir until the *polenta* is thick and pulls away easily from the sides of the pan with the spoon. If the *polenta* is quite thick but still not pulling, add a little more boiling water and continue to stir until it is ready. It should be perfectly cooked, thick, and creamy in 25 to 30 minutes and can then be used. Proceed with any of the following *polenta antipasti.*

INSALATA DI FAGIOLI ALLA BANDIERA

BEAN SALAD WITH ROASTED RED PEPPERS, ONION, MARJORAM, AND LEMON

FOR 4 PEOPLE

❋

THE *bandiera*, OR "FLAG," SYMBOLIZED IN THIS DISH IS THE RED, GREEN AND WHITE BANNER OF ITALY. THE SECRET TO THIS DELICIOUS SALAD IS TO USE FRESH MARJORAM OR THYME. IF THIS ISN'T POSSIBLE, SUBSTITUTE DRIED MARJORAM OR THYME, BUT BE SURE TO MARINATE IT IN THE DRESSING BEFORE ADDING IT TO THE BEANS.

* *1-½ cups dried cannellini or Great Northern beans, or 3 cups drained canned white beans*
* *1 fresh red sweet pepper, or ½ cup bottled red sweet peppers, well drained*
* *⅓ pound green beans, trimmed and cut into 1-inch lengths*
* *1 tablespoon freshly squeezed lemon juice*
* *¼ cup extra-virgin olive oil*
* *1 tablespoon chopped fresh marjoram or thyme, or ½ teaspoon dried marjoram or thyme*
* *2 green onions, white part only, very thinly sliced*
* *salt and freshly milled black pepper*
* *scant 1 tablespoon chopped fresh Italian parsley*

❶ SOAK AND COOK the dried beans as directed on page 7. Drain well. You will have about 3 cups cooked beans; set aside. If using canned beans, rinse them briefly in cold water and drain well. Roast the fresh sweet pepper according to directions on page 27. When the pepper is cool enough to handle, slip off the skin, cut the pepper in half, and remove and discard the stem, ribs, and seeds. Cut the fresh roasted pepper or the bottled peppers, if using, into ½-inch squares.

❷ MEANWHILE, fill a saucepan with salted water and bring to a boil. Add the green beans (the salt will help them to retain their color) and boil until tender but still firm, about 7 minutes. As soon as they are cooked, plunge them into cold water. Drain well.

❸ TO MAKE THE DRESSING, in a small bowl stir together the lemon juice and oil. If you are using dried marjoram or thyme, add it to the dressing. Combine the white beans, sweet pepper, green beans, fresh marjoram or thyme, and green onions in a serving bowl. Add the dressing and salt and pepper to taste and toss well. Sprinkle on the parsley and serve at room temperature.

SFORMATO DI POLENTA E VERDURA

POLENTA AND VEGETABLE MOLD

FOR 8 TO 10 PEOPLE

❊

Lidia Bastianich, who, with her husband, Felice, owns the excellent Felidia Ristorante in New York City, gave me the idea for making a mold using *polenta* and vegetables. She combines cooked shrimp and all kinds of vegetables for a lovely terrazzo effect. You can be very creative with this. My favorite variation is to fold in whole grilled or sautéed wild mushrooms and poached, sliced artichoke hearts because they both go so well with the nutty flavor of corn *polenta*. Because the mushrooms are folded in whole, they must not be too large; select mushrooms that are not much bigger than two inches in diameter. Try using either the mushrooms or the artichoke hearts alone, if you like. If using only mushrooms, one-half pound will do; if using only artichoke hearts, increase the number to three. Just remember, frozen or canned artichokes hearts are not a good substitute. Once the vegetables are folded into the *polenta*, the mixture is poured into a loaf pan and cooled. It is unmolded, sliced, brushed with extra-virgin olive oil, and broiled, grilled, or fried.

* *2 artichokes (about ½ pound each)*
* *½ pound fresh wild mushrooms such as* shiitake, chanterelle, *or* cremini
* *extra-virgin olive oil as needed*
* *1 recipe Basic* Polenta *(page 91)*

❊❊❊

❶ Trim, boil, and slice the artichokes as directed on page 53.

❷ Preheat a broiler or indoor grill, or prepare a fire in a charcoal grill. Remove any dirt from the mushrooms with a soft brush or dry cotton towel. Trim off the hard tips of the stems; if the stems are tough, discard them. Leave the mushrooms whole and brush them with olive oil. Place on a grill rack or arrange them on a baking sheet and slip under a broiler. Sear the mushrooms on all sides. This should take only a couple of minutes.

❸ Alternatively, in a skillet, preferably nonstick, warm 2 tablespoons olive oil over high heat. Add the mushrooms and sauté briefly to sear them; do not let the mushrooms reduce too much. Lift out the mushrooms with a slotted utensil and set aside. Pour off the pan juices.

❹ In the same skillet, warm 2 tablespoons olive oil over medium heat. Add the artichokes and sauté, turning once, until browned lightly on both sides, 8 to 10 minutes. Lift out the artichokes with a slotted utensil and set aside. Rub a 5-by-9-by-3-inch loaf pan with olive oil and set aside.

❺ Make the *polenta* as directed. When it is almost ready to be removed from the burner, add the seared mushrooms and sautéed artichokes. Stir them in well to distribute evenly throughout the *polenta;* if you do not, air pockets will form and make slicing difficult. Immediately pour the hot *polenta* into the prepared loaf pan. Use a rubber spatula to remove any *polenta* that clings to the pan and to smooth the top of the mold. Let cool at room temperature for 3 to 4 hours.

❻ Turn the loaf pan upside down onto a cutting board and lift off the pan. Using a sharp knife, cut the mold into ½ inch-thick slices. To broil or grill the slices, preheat a broiler or inside grill, or prepare a fire in a charcoal grill.

❼ If broiling the slices, brush them generously on both sides with olive oil and arrange them on an oiled baking sheet. Slip them under a broiler about 8 inches from the heat source. Broil, turning once, until golden and crisp on both sides, 10 to 15 minutes' total cooking time. If using an indoor or outdoor grill, place the slices, first brushed generously with olive oil, about ½ inch apart, directly on the grill over heat source or coals. Grill, turning once with a metal spatula, until browned on both sides.

Alternatively, pour olive oil into a large skillet, preferably nonstick, to a depth of ½ inch and heat until a small piece of *polenta* sizzles the instant it is dropped into it. When the oil is ready, slip the slices, a few at a time, into the pan and fry, turning once, until golden on both sides, 10 to 12 minutes. Lift out with a slotted utensil and drain on paper towels. Repeat with the remaining slices, adding more oil to the pan as needed and heating it to the proper temperature before adding more *polenta* slices. Serve the *polenta* slices piping hot.

FAGIOLI CON SALSICCIA E POMODORO MODO DI MIA MAMMA

MY MOTHER'S BEANS WITH SAUSAGE AND TOMATO

FOR 4 PEOPLE

HOT BEAN DISHES ARE ONE OF THOSE *antipasti* THAT CAN APPEAR ANYWHERE IN THE COURSE OF THE MEAL: AS A STARTER, AS A FIRST COURSE, AS A MAIN COURSE, OR AS A *contorno*. IT IS SAFE TO SAY THAT THIS WAY OF COOKING BEANS IS PAN-ITALIAN; CERTAINLY ONE FINDS IT IN TUSCANY, IN LAZIO (ROME), AND IN MANY SOUTHERN REGIONS. UNFORTUNATELY, THE BEANS THAT ARE AVAILABLE HERE HAVE LITTLE FLAVOR. WHEN I WAS GROWING UP, MY MOTHER ALWAYS REMINISCED ABOUT THE THINGS SHE MISSED FROM ITALY (SHE STILL DOES). THE FLAVOR OF ITALIAN BEANS WAS ONE OF THEM. I HAVE FRIENDS WHO CARRY BEANS BACK FROM TUSCANY—THE HOME OF TRUE BEAN LOVERS—WHEN THEY GO THERE BECAUSE THE BEANS ARE SO FLAVORFUL. SOME OF THE SAME TYPES OF BEANS ARE AVAILABLE HERE—LENTILS AND *cannellini* BEANS, FOR EXAMPLE—BUT SOMEHOW THEIR FLAVOR PALES IN COMPARISON. NEVERTHELESS, IN A RECIPE SUCH AS THIS, THE SAUCE AND SUCCULENT FENNEL SAUSAGES GIVE GREAT FLAVOR TO THE BEANS, AND IT IS ALTOGETHER A FABULOUS DISH.

* 1-1/2 cups dried cannellini or Great Northern beans, or 3 cups drained canned white beans
* salt to taste, plus ½ teaspoon
* 2 tablespoons extra-virgin olive oil
* 1 onion, finely chopped
* 1 clove garlic, finely chopped
* 3 sweet Italian fennel sausages (about ½ pound total weight), casings removed
* 1 tablespoon tomato paste
* 3 fresh sage leaves, cut into thin strips, or ½ teaspoon dried sage
* ½ cup beef stock or water
* freshly milled black pepper
* 1 tablespoon chopped fresh Italian parsley

❶ WASH AND PICK OVER the dried beans. Put them in a pot and add cold water to cover by 3 inches. Let stand overnight at room temperature. Alternatively, quick-soak the dried beans by putting them in a saucepan with water to cover by 3 inches. Bring to a boil, cover, remove from the heat, and let stand for 1 hour.

❷ DRAIN THE SOAKED BEANS and put them in a pot with 3 inches of fresh cold water to cover. Bring to a boil and immediately reduce to a simmer. Cook gently until the beans are tender but not falling apart, about 1 hour. Salt the beans only after cooking, or they will toughen. Drain the beans. You will have about 3 cups cooked beans. If using canned beans, rinse them briefly in cold water and drain well.

❸ IN A SKILLET over medium-low heat, warm the olive oil. Add the onion and garlic and sauté gently until totally softened but not browned, about 5 minutes. Using a slotted spoon, remove the onion and garlic from the pan and transfer to a small dish.

❹ REMOVE ANY EXCESS fat from the sausage, if possible. Heat the oil that remains in the pan and add the sausage meat to it, crumbling it and breaking it up with a wooden spoon. Sauté, stirring, until browned, about 5 minutes. Return the onion and garlic to the pan. Add the tomato paste, sage, stock or water, the ½ teaspoon salt, and pepper to taste. Bring to a boil. Add the beans. Bring to a boil again and immediately reduce to a simmer. Partially cover and cook gently for 10 to 15 minutes. Sprinkle with the parsley. Serve hot or warm.

FAGIOLI ALL'UCCELLETTO

TUSCAN "BEANS LIKE BIRDS"

FOR 4 PEOPLE

❋

THIS FAMOUS TUSCAN DISH CAN BE SERVED AS AN *antipasto* OR AS A SIDE DISH WITH MEAT.

* *1 cup dried cannellini or Great Northern beans,*
  or 2 cups canned white beans with liquid
* *½ pound ripe plum tomatoes or other vine-ripened tomatoes,*
  or ½ cup canned plum tomatoes, drained, seeded, and chopped
* *¼ cup extra-virgin olive oil*
* *1 large clove garlic, bruised*
* *2 teaspoons chopped fresh sage leaves, or 1 teaspoon dried sage*
* *¼ teaspoon salt*
* *¼ teaspoon freshly milled black pepper*

❶ SOAK AND COOK beans as directed on page 96. Drain them when they are just tender, and reserve ⅓ cup of their cooking liquid. You will have about 2 cups cooked beans. If using canned beans, drain them, reserving ⅓ cup of their liquid, then rinse them briefly in cold water and drain well. (If the liquid does not measure ⅓ cup, add water as needed.)

❷ IF USING FRESH TOMATOES, bring a saucepan filled with water to a boil, add the tomatoes, and blanch for 30 seconds. Remove from the water and, when cool enough to handle, peel them and cut in half crosswise. Remove and discard their seeds, and then cut into medium dice. You will have about ½ cup; set aside.

❸ IN A LARGE SKILLET over medium-low heat, warm together the olive oil and garlic until the garlic colors, 6 or 7 minutes. Add the beans and reserved cooking liquid, sage, salt, and pepper and simmer for 4 to 5 minutes. Add the tomatoes and stir to distribute. Heat through for 2 to 3 minutes. Remove and discard the garlic. Serve hot or at room temperature.

INSALATA DI LENTICCHIE COL FINOCCHIO

LENTIL SALAD WITH FENNEL

FOR 4 PEOPLE

❋

LENTILS ARE DELICIOUS NOT ONLY HOT, BUT ALSO COLD IN SALADS. THE ANISEY SWEETNESS OF FENNEL CONTRASTS NICELY WITH THE EARTHINESS OF THE LENTILS, AND THE OAKY MELLOWNESS OF THE BALSAMIC VINEGAR IN THE DRESSING MARRIES THE DIFFERENT FLAVORS IN A SATISFYING WAY. IF FRESH FENNEL IS NOT AVAILABLE, CELERY AND CHOPPED CELERY LEAVES, OR RAW RED OR YELLOW BELL PEPPERS CAN BE SUBSTITUTED.

* *1 cup dried brown lentils*
* *2 tablespoons extra-virgin olive oil*
* *2 tablespoons balsamic vinegar*
* *1 small fennel bulb (about 6 ounces),*
  trimmed, with leaves reserved, and julienned
* *1 teaspoon chopped fresh thyme, or*
  ½ teaspoon dried thyme
* *2 green onions, white part only, very*
  thinly sliced
* *1 teaspoon salt, or to taste*
* *¼ teaspoon freshly milled black pepper, or to taste*
* *1 tablespoon thinly sliced fresh chives or*
  tops of green onions

❶ WASH AND PICK OVER the lentils, discarding any discolored ones. Put them in a saucepan and add cold water to cover by 3 inches. Bring the water to a boil and reduce immediately to a simmer. Cook until the lentils are tender but still firm, about 15 minutes. Drain them immediately and rinse them with cold water. Drain again.

❷ IN A SERVING BOWL, stir together the oil and vinegar. Add the lentils and toss to coat. Add the fennel, thyme, white part of green onions, salt, and pepper. Taste and adjust for seasonings. Sprinkle the salad with the chives or green onion tops. Chop the reserved fennel leaves to measure 1 tablespoon and sprinkle over the top. Serve warm or at room temperature.

GAMBERI E FAGIOLI CANNELLINI ALLA TOSCANA

TUSCAN-STYLE SHRIMP AND CANNELLINI BEANS

FOR 4 OR 5 PEOPLE

HERE IS AN ADAPTATION OF A MARVELOUS DISH I HAVE HAD IN TUSCANY, WHERE IT IS MADE WITH THE SMALL LOCAL SHRIMP. IT IS BEST WHEN PREPARED WITH FRESH TOMATOES, WHICH HOLD THEIR SHAPE AND TEXTURE BETTER. THE TOMATOES SHOULD NOT STEW INTO A SAUCE. THEY MUST STAND OUT AS A SEPARATE ELEMENT IN THE DISH, AND SO ARE COOKED ONLY VERY BRIEFLY. I PREFER THE DISH MADE WITH DRIED BEANS BECAUSE THEY, TOO, HOLD THEIR SHAPE AND TEXTURE BETTER THAN THEIR CANNED COUNTERPART. CANNED BEANS CAN BE SUBSTITUTED, HOWEVER.

* *1 cup dried* cannellini *or Great Northern beans, or 2 cups canned white beans with liquid*
* *1 clove garlic, unpeeled, bruised*
* *1 bay leaf*
* *1 pound ripe plum tomatoes or other vine-ripened tomatoes, or 1 cup canned plum tomatoes, drained, seeded, and chopped*
* *¾ pound shrimp, peeled and deveined*
* *6 tablespoons extra-virgin olive oil*
* *2 large cloves garlic, finely chopped, plus 1 clove garlic, bruised*
* *2 tablespoons fresh basil leaves, torn into small pieces or chopped, plus whole leaves for garnish*
* *2 teaspoons chopped fresh Italian parsley*
* *1-⅛ teaspoons salt, or to taste*
* *¼ teaspoon freshly milled black pepper, or to taste*

❶ SOAK AND COOK beans as directed on page 96, adding the unpeeled garlic clove and bay leaf to the cooking water. Drain them when they are just tender and reserve ½ cup of the cooking liquid. You will have about 2 cups cooked beans; set aside. If using canned beans, drain them, reserving ⅓ cup of their liquid, then rinse them briefly in cold water and drain well. Add enough water to the bean liquid to measure ½ cup. Set the beans and liquid aside.

❷ IF USING FRESH TOMATOES, bring a saucepan filled with water to a boil, add the tomatoes, and blanch for 30 seconds. Remove from the water and, when cool enough to handle, peel them and cut in half crosswise. Remove and discard their seeds, and then cut into medium dice. You will have about 1 cup; set aside.

❸ DRY THE SHRIMP with a cotton kitchen towel. Heat 4 tablespoons of the oil in a large skillet and add the shrimp. If you are using canned beans, add the bay leaf to the shrimp in the skillet at this point, and omit the unpeeled garlic clove from the recipe. Sauté until the shrimp are almost cooked, about 2 minutes on each side. Now add the chopped garlic, torn or chopped basil, parsley, beans and the reserved cooking liquid (if using canned beans, add them and their reserved diluted liquid), salt, and pepper. Heat through, about 2 minutes.

❹ IN ANOTHER PAN, heat 1 tablespoon of the remaining oil with the bruised garlic clove and sauté until the garlic is golden. Add the tomatoes and sauté quickly for 1 minute. Remove and discard the garlic. Add the tomatoes to the shrimp and beans. If the bay leaf was added to the shrimp, remove and discard it now. Taste for salt and pepper. Drizzle the remaining 1 tablespoon oil over the dish. Garnish with whole basil leaves. Serve hot or warm.

FAGIOLI CON PANCETTA E SALVIA

STEWED LIMA BEANS WITH TOMATOES, BACON, PARSLEY, AND GREEN ONIONS, LATIUM STYLE

FOR 4 PEOPLE

❋

THIS WAY OF COOKING BEANS IS TYPICAL OF LAZIO, OF WHICH ROME IS THE CAPITAL CITY. THERE, THE DISH IS CALLED *fagioli al corallo* BECAUSE OF THE CORAL-SPECKLED BEANS THAT ARE USED. WE CANNOT EASILY FIND THAT VARIETY HERE. DRIED BABY LIMA BEANS ARE A GOOD SUBSTITUTE, HOWEVER. ANY KIND OF HAM, BACON, OR *pancetta* HAS A GREAT AFFINITY WITH BEANS; IF *pancetta* IS NOT AVAILABLE, USE THICKLY SLICED LEAN BACON.

❋ *1 cup dried baby lima beans*
❋ *2 tablespoons extra-virgin olive oil*
❋ *2 ounces* pancetta, *trimmed of excess fat and diced, or 2 slices lean bacon, diced*
❋ *1 clove garlic, bruised*
❋ *2 green onions, white part and 1 inch of green, sliced*
❋ *4 fresh sage leaves, or ½ teaspoon dried sage*
❋ *5 large cherry tomatoes, seeded and coarsely chopped*
❋ *1-½ teaspoons salt, or to taste*
❋ *½ teaspoon freshly milled black pepper*
❋ *¼ cup water*
❋ *2 tablespoons chopped fresh Italian parsley*

❶ SOAK AND COOK beans as directed on page 96. When cooking the lima beans, keep in mind to simmer them gently; they have a tendency to disintegrate if not cooked delicately. Remove from the heat when they are tender but still firm, and drain immediately. Do not rinse them, but set them aside to cool.

❷ IN A SKILLET over medium-low heat, warm the olive oil. Add the *pancetta* or bacon and sauté until it colors, about 5 minutes. Using a slotted utensil transfer the *pancetta* or bacon to a small dish and set aside. To the same oil, add the garlic and green onions and sauté just until softened, about 2 minutes. Add the sage, tomatoes, salt, pepper, and the reserved *pancetta* or bacon and sauté for another 2 minutes. Add the beans and the water. Stir to mix, then cover and cook over low heat, stirring occasionally, for 10 minutes. Sprinkle with the parsley and serve hot.

CROSTINI DI POLENTA

POLENTA TOASTS

MAKES APPROXIMATELY 30 CROSTINI; FOR 6 OR 7 PEOPLE

❋

Polenta CAN BE FRIED, BROILED, OR GRILLED TO FORM SMALL *crostini*. THERE ARE MANY THINGS TO DO WITH THESE NUTTY-FLAVORED, CRISPY TOASTS. THEY ARE LOVELY SERVED WITH SAUTÉED WILD MUSHROOMS, SEE PAGE 48, OR WITH THE CHICKEN LIVER SPREAD ON PAGE 67. GRILLED *crostini* ARE PARTICULARLY NICE TOPPED WITH A THIN SLICE OF *fontina* OR AN UNADORNED MOUND OF CAVIAR. OTHER NICE TOPPINGS ARE TUNA BUTTER, *gorgonzola* BUTTER, CAVIAR BUTTER, OR SMOKED SALMON BUTTER (PAGE 132). LITTLE SANDWICHES CAN BE MADE WITH THESE CORNMEAL *crostini* USING *prosciutto* AND OTHER SLICED CURED MEATS (*affettati*), OR USING SEMISOFT CHEESES SUCH AS *stracchino, fontina, taleggio,* AND *gorgonzola*.

❋ *olive oil or vegetable oil for oiling board*
❋ *1 recipe Basic* Polenta *(page 91)*

FOR FRYING:
❋ *extra-virgin olive oil*
❋ *all-purpose flour for dredging*

FOR BROILING OR GRILLING:
❋ *melted unsalted butter or extra-virgin olive oil for brushing on* polenta *squares and rubbing on baking sheet*

❶ USING OLIVE OIL or vegetable oil, lightly oil 2 large pastry boards or a very large, scratch-proof counter surface. Make the *polenta* as directed. When it is cooked, pour it out onto the boards or counter surface. Using a knife that has first been dipped into cold water to prevent the *polenta* from sticking to it, spread it into a disk or rectangle approximately ¼ inch thick. Leave to set until completely cool and firm, about 15 minutes.

❷ USING A KNIFE, cut the cooled, hardened *polenta* into 2-½-inch squares, or cut on the diagonal to form diamond shapes

❸ TO FRY THE SQUARES, pour olive oil into a large skillet, preferably nonstick, to a depth of ½ inch and heat until a corner of a *polenta* square sizzles the instant it is dropped into it. Meanwhile, dust the squares with flour. When the oil is ready, slip the squares into the pan and fry over medium heat, turning once, until golden on both sides, about 5 minutes per side. Lift out with a slotted utensil and drain on paper towels.

❹ TO BROIL OR GRILL the *polenta* squares, preheat a broiler or indoor grill, or prepare a fire in a charcoal grill. Brush the *polenta* squares on both sides with melted butter or olive oil and place them, about ½ inch apart, on an oiled baking sheet. Slip them under the broiler, turning once, until browned on both sides, about 3 minutes on each side. If using an indoor or outdoor grill, place them, about ½ inch apart, directly on the grill over heat source or coals, turning once with a metal spatula, until browned on both sides.

❺ SERVE THE SQUARES hot. If, however, you are spreading any of the blended butters on the fried, broiled, or grilled *crostini*, let the squares cool slightly so that the butter in the spreads does not melt instantly.

PANISSA

LIGURIAN CHICK-PEA FLOUR POLENTA

FOR 6 TO 8 PEOPLE

❋

THIS INTERESTING VARIATION ON *polenta* IS MADE WITH CHICK-PEA FLOUR RATHER THAN CORNMEAL. THERE IS NO SIMILARITY IN FLAVOR BETWEEN *polenta* AND *panissa*, HOWEVER. CHICK-PEA FLOUR HAS A BOLDER FLAVOR, AND WHEREAS POLENTA MADE FROM CORN IS PLEASANTLY GRITTY, THE TEXTURE OF *panissa* IS VERY SOFT. FRIED IN EXTRA-VIRGIN OLIVE OIL, PANISSA IS GOLDEN AND CRISP ON THE OUTSIDE AND ALMOST CREAMY WITHIN. ❋ *Panissa*, A LIGURIAN SPECIALTY, IS TYPICALLY SERVED WITH *bottarga*, A COMPRESSED CAVIAR OF MULLET EGGS MUCH BELOVED BY THE LIGURIANS AND THE SARDINIANS. *Bottarga* IS NOT EXPORTED TO THE UNITED STATES, BUT FRESH CAVIAR WILL DO SPLENDIDLY. I EVEN LIKE THESE LITTLE FRIED CHICK-PEA SQUARES PLAIN AS A SNACK, AND SOMETIMES I SERVE THEM AS A SIDE DISH WITH ROASTED OR GRILLED MEAT. THEY ARE AN ESPECIALLY SUCCESSFUL COMPLEMENTARY APPETIZER WITH *spiedini di agnello con limone* (PAGE 64).

* *olive oil or vegetable oil for oiling board*
* *3-½ cups water*
* *2 teaspoons salt*
* *2 cups chick-pea flour*
* *extra-virgin olive oil for frying*
* *4 ounces caviar*

❶ USING OLIVE OIL or vegetable oil, lightly oil a large pastry board approximately 12 by 18 inches or two smaller ones. Have a rubber spatula ready for spreading the *panissa* on the board when it is cooked. Pour the water into a saucepan and add the salt. Gradually add the chick-pea flour, whisking constantly to mix it in thoroughly. Bring the mixture to a boil, stirring constantly with the whisk to prevent lumps from forming. Reduce the heat to medium and continue to stir constantly with the whisk until the mixture is as thick as porridge or *polenta,* 20 to 30 minutes. Remove it from the burner and immediately turn it out onto the oiled pastry board(s), using a spatula dipped in cold water to spread it out over the surface of the board(s) to a thickness of about 1/4 inch. Allow to cool for 20 to 30 minutes.

❷ WHEN IT IS SOLID enough to cut easily, cut it into 2-½-inch squares with a sharp knife. Pour enough extra-virgin olive oil into a large skillet, preferably nonstick, to cover the bottom of the pan generously, and heat until it is almost smoking. When the oil is ready, slip the squares, a few at a time, into the pan and fry over medium heat until golden on both sides, about 5 minutes per side. Lift out with a slotted utensil and drain on paper towels.

❸ SERVE HOT or at room temperature. Top each square with about 1 teaspoon of the caviar. Eat immediately.

AHEAD-OF-TIME NOTE: *Panissa* can be made 2 or 3 days in advance and refrigerated before frying. It will release water once refrigerated, however, and must be patted dry thoroughly so that it will take on a crisp exterior when fried. Alternatively, make and fry the *panissa* squares 4 to 5 hours in advance and set them aside at room temperature. To reheat them, place the squares, about ½ inch apart, on a baking sheet and bake in an oven preheated to 375 degrees F for 8 to 10 minutes.

Chapter 7

SAVORY BREADS, PIES, & SANDWICHES

Pane, crostate, e tramezzini

A SEPARATE book would be required to explore this category of *antipasti* thoroughly. The *Italian Baker* by Carol Field is a seminal source for *focaccie, pizze,* and breads of all sorts, and so is Elizabeth Romer's *Italian Pizze and Hearth-breads. Pizza* is the southern term, while *focaccia* in the north and *schiacciata* in Tuscany stand for essentially the same primitive flat bread. When these breads are offered as *antipasti,* they are miniature versions of their usual size, and their variety is immense. ❋ Although they are most commonly made with wheat flour, these flatbreads are sometimes composed of *polenta* (cornmeal), chick-pea flour, boiled potatoes, and, less frequently, chestnut flour. Their toppings might include caramelized onions, seafood, *prosciutto,* tomatoes, rosemary and other herbs, and many different cheeses, from *mozzarella* to *gorgonzola, parmigiano,* and *pecorino.* Some *focaccie* are stuffed, such as a Ligurian one filled with *stracchino* cheese, or a Sardinian specialty packed with minced pork and sun-dried tomatoes. Also in this category are the fried and baked turnovers called *calzoni, calzoncelli, pizzelle,* or *frittelle,* among other names. These are usually stuffed with ham, *salame,* or *ricotta* or other soft fresh cheeses. I have chosen not to elaborate extensively on such breads in this volume on *antipasti,* but included are the basic doughs for *pizza* and *frittelle* with which the reader can improvise his or her own versions. ❋ Besides flat breads, there are a number of savory pies, tarts, and pastries that fit into the *antipasto* category. The delicate *torte* of Genoa included in this chapter are made with puff pastry. Most of Italy's savory pies, from the earthy chick-pea flour *farinata* of Liguria to the onion and anchovy pie of Apulian origin that appear here, are rustic dishes. ❋ *Grissini,* or "breadsticks," are often placed on the table before an Italian meal begins. They need not be the innocuous, mass-produced variety that is often found in little plastic packages on the tables of Italian restaurants in America. Italian bakers roll and cut these superb breads into long *bastoni,* or "sticks," by hand. When they come out

of the oven they are gnarled, golden brown, and crunchy–lovely for nibbling on while sipping a glass of wine before a meal, or to use as a mast around which to wrap paper-thin, rosy *prosciutto*. ❀ Probably the humblest of the *antipasti* in the bread category is *bruschetta*, which is called *fettunta* in Tuscany and is so simple as to need no formal instructions. Traditionally, thick slices of bread are toasted over an open fire, rubbed with plenty of garlic while they are still warm, drizzled generously with the first *spremuta*–"squeezing"–of the new season's olive oil and then sprinkled with sea salt. The slices should be thick to prevent them from drying out and falling apart when they are rubbed with the garlic. If you do not have a grill going, the bread can be toasted in the oven. While such a *bruschetta* does not have the romance of the ritualistic toasting of bread and pouring of the new season's first drops of precious olive oil, it is still delicious. In the summer, when sweet, vine-ripened tomatoes are available, they are sometimes chopped and mixed with basil and the same good oil and spread over the *bruschetta*. A variation of *bruschetta* from Apulia is *frisa*, in which slabs of peasant bread are toasted over the fire, drizzled with the local fruity green olive oil, and topped with finely sliced sweet onions and chopped fresh tomatoes. ❀ *Crostini* are among the most popular of the bread-based *antipasti*. These are nothing more than little rounds of toasted bread topped with any of a number of spreads, for which recipes appear in various chapters (see chapter 4 for a chicken liver spread, and chapter 8 for other spreads and butters). They may also be topped with cheese, such as the pizzalike Neapolitan *crostini* that are piled with *mozzarella*, anchovy, chopped tomato, oregano, and salt, and baked until the cheese melts. Typically found in Roman *pizzerie* are *crostini col prosciutto*, toasted bread topped with *prosciutto* and *mozzarella* and then placed briefly in a wood-burning oven. ❀ ❀ ❀

TORTA PASQUALINA

GENOESE EASTER TART

FOR 8 PEOPLE

❋

THIS SAVORY *antipasto* PASTRY IS MADE IN GENOA AT EASTER TIME. THE STUFFING IS THE CLASSIC MIXTURE OF SPINACH OR SWISS CHARD, *ricotta, parmigiano,* AND NUTMEG THAT GOES INTO *ravioli.* ANOTHER VARIATION ALSO CHARACTERISTIC OF GENOA IS *torta di carciofi,* MADE WITH ARTICHOKE HEARTS SAUTÉED WITH ONION, PARSLEY, MARJORAM, AND *parmigiano,* AND COMBINED WITH *latte cagliato,* A KIND OF CLOTTED CREAM. IT IS AN OLD CUSTOM IN GENOA THAT THE PUFF PASTRY DOUGH SHOULD HAVE TWENTY *sfoglie,* OR "LAYERS." IN SAVONA, THERE ARE THIRTY-THREE, TO REPRESENT THE AGE OF CHRIST. TODAY, ONLY SEVEN OR EIGHT LAYERS ARE USED. ONCE THE FILLING IS PREPARED, THE PROCEDURE FOR MAKING THE TART IS THE SAME AS THAT FOR SAUSAGE AND MUSHROOM TART (PAGE 111).

FOR THE FILLING:
* ❋ *1 pound spinach or Swiss chard, stemmed*
* ❋ *1-¼ cups* ricotta, *placed in a sieve for 1 to 2 hours to drain excess liquid*
* ❋ *1 egg yolk*
* ❋ *⅛ teaspoon freshly grated nutmeg*
* ❋ *¼ teaspoon salt*
* ❋ *5 tablespoons freshly grated* parmigiano
* ❋ *freshly milled black pepper*

* ❋ *1 pound puff pastry, chilled*
* ❋ *1 egg, lightly beaten with 1 tablespoon milk*
* ❋ *unsalted butter for greasing baking sheet (optional)*

❶ PREHEAT AN OVEN to 425 degrees F. To make the filling, place the spinach or chard in a saucepan without the addition of any more water than the drops still clinging to the leaves from washing. Cover and cook over medium heat until tender, just a few minutes. Remove from the heat, let cool, and then, using your hands, squeeze out as much water as you can. Chop finely and place in a bowl. Add all the remaining filling ingredients, including pepper to taste, and mix well. Set aside.

❷ PLACE THE PUFF PASTRY on a lightly floured pastry board and roll it out lightly just to smooth out the creases. Cut it in half horizontally so that you have 2 squares or rectangles (the shape will depend upon the size of the premade pastry). Place the filling in the middle of one of the pastry sheets, leaving a 1-inch border on all sides. Brush the border with some of the egg-milk mixture. Place the second sheet of pastry on top and crimp the edges well all around with a fork to seal. Brush the top with more of the egg-milk mixture.

❸ TRANSFER TO A parchment-lined baking sheet or a baking sheet that has been lightly greased with butter. Bake in the preheated oven until golden brown, 15 to 20 minutes. Remove to a rack and allow to settle for 5 to 10 minutes. Cut into squares and serve hot.

PIZZADALINA

ONION PIZZA, APULIA STYLE

MAKES ONE 12-INCH ROUND PIZZA OR TWO 6-INCH ROUND PIZZAS; FOR 4 TO 6 PEOPLE

✳

MY PATERNAL GRANDMOTHER, WHO WAS BORN IN APULIA, MADE THIS PIE. FOR MY FATHER, IT BECAME A DISH THAT, LIKE SO MANY IMMIGRANT FOODS, WAS IMBUED WITH SYMBOLIC MEANING FAR BEYOND PROVIDING NOURISHMENT AND PLEASURE. IT WAS AS THOUGH ITS APPEARANCE ON THE TABLE—ITS AROMA AND ITS EARTHY, FAMILIAR TASTE—WAS A LINK TO THE PAST. MY FATHER, NOW IN HIS EIGHTY-FOURTH YEAR, STILL TALKS ABOUT HIS MOTHER'S ONION PIE AS THOUGH IN RECALLING IT HE RECALLS HER AND THE BELOVED ITALY THAT WAS LEFT BEHIND. THIS SOUTHERN FLAT BREAD IS A LOVELY THING TO SERVE BEFORE DINNER WITH WINE OR AS A SNACK OR LIGHT LUNCH. IT MIGHT ALSO APPEAR WITH THE MAIN COURSE, PARTICULARLY IF PORK OR FOWL IS BEING SERVED. THE FINELY SLICED ONIONS ARE COOKED VERY SLOWLY UNTIL THEY CARAMELIZE, WHICH RENDERS THEM VERY SWEET—A LOVELY CONTRAST TO THE SHARP BLACK OLIVES, SALTY SOUTHERN *pecorino*, AND PUNGENT OREGANO.

* ½ recipe pizza dough for Classic Neapolitan Pizza, page 118
* extra-virgin olive oil for oiling pans, if using
* cornmeal for baker's peel, if using
* 3 tablespoons extra-virgin olive oil
* 2 large cloves garlic, bruised
* 1 pound onions, cut into quarters and thinly sliced
* 1 bay leaf
* 1 tablespoon chopped fresh oregano, or 1-½ teaspoons dried oregano
* ½ teaspoon salt
* freshly milled black pepper
* ¼ cup freshly grated pecorino
* ¼ cup pitted and sliced, sharp-flavored black Italian olives

❶ MAKE THE PIZZA DOUGH as directed through the first rising. If you are using a pizza pan, preheat an oven to 400 degrees F. If using a baking stone or terra-cotta tiles, place in the oven and preheat to 450 degrees F for 40 minutes.

❷ CONTINUING TO FOLLOW the recipe, punch down the dough. (If you wish to make 2 pizzas, divide the dough in half at this point.) Roll out the dough ¼ inch to ½ inch thick. If you are using a pan for the pizza, oil it before pressing the dough out in it. If you are using a baker's peel, sprinkle it with cornmeal before placing the rolled-out dough on it. (In the absence of a peel, dust a baking sheet without sides with cornmeal.) Cover the pizza base with a towel and let rise in a warm place undisturbed for 30 minutes.

❸ WHILE THE DOUGH is rising, in a large skillet over low heat, warm the oil and garlic together until the garlic is golden, 5 to 7 minutes. Add the onions, bay leaf, and oregano and sauté gently until the onions are very soft but not browned, about 15 minutes. Add the salt and pepper to taste. Remove and discard the garlic and bay leaf. Allow the onion mixture to cool somewhat, then spread it over the risen pizza base and sprinkle with the cheese. Strew the olives over the top. Brush the edges of the crust with olive oil.

❹ IF USING A PIZZA PAN, bake the pizza in the preheated oven until the edges are golden, about 20 minutes. If using a baking stone or tiles, slide the pizza off the peel (or baking sheet) directly onto the heated surface. Bake until the edges are golden, 15 to 20 minutes. Allow to settle for 5 minutes before cutting. Use a pastry wheel to cut the pizza into wedges. Eat hot or warm.

VARIATIONS: Add 6 anchovy fillets in olive oil, drained and cut up, or 2 ounces *pancetta* or bacon, diced, lightly sautéed, and drained on paper towels, with the olives.

PIZZA RIPIENA

FILLED PIZZA

FOR 8 TO 10 PEOPLE

❋

THE MAKING OF THIS RUSTIC, SAVORY PIE IS AN EASTER RITUAL IN MANY NEAPOLITAN HOUSEHOLDS. THE RECIPE THAT FOLLOWS INCLUDES DIRECTIONS FOR A LIGHT, FLAKY SHORT CRUST, OR YOU CAN MAKE YOUR OWN FAVORITE SUGARLESS PIE CRUST.

FOR THE CRUST:
* *1-¾ cups unbleached all-purpose flour, chilled*
* *½ teaspoon salt*
* *½ cup lard or unsalted butter, or a combination, chilled*
* *½ cup ice water*

FOR THE FILLING:
* *4 extra-large eggs*
* *¾ pound (1-½ cups)* ricotta
* *¼ teaspoon salt*
* *¼ pound thinly sliced cooked ham, cut into ½-inch dice and dusted with a little flour*
* *2 ounces thinly sliced* soppressata *or other Italian* salame, *cut into ½-inch dice and tossed with a little flour*
* *¼ pound* mozzarella, *cut into ½-inch dice*
* *¼ cup freshly grated* parmigiano
* *freshly milled black pepper*

* *unsalted butter for greasing pan*
* *all-purpose flour for dusting pan and board*
* *1 egg white, lightly beaten*
* *1 egg yolk and a pinch of salt for egg wash*

❶ TO MAKE THE CRUST, stir together the flour and salt in a mixing bowl. Using a pastry blender or 2 knives, cut in the lard or butter until kidney bean–shaped lumps form. Sprinkle the ice water over the top of the mixture, then work the water throughout the mixture by gently tossing with 2 forks. Using your hands, form 2 balls of dough, one twice as large as the other; be careful not to overhandle the dough. Put the dough in a loosely covered bowl or plastic bag, leaving room for a little air to enter. Chill for 2 hours.

❷ PREHEAT AN OVEN to 375 degrees F. To make the filling, in a bowl beat the eggs until thick and pale. Beat in the *ricotta* until well incorporated, then mix in the salt, ham, *soppressata, mozzarella, parmigiano,* and pepper to taste. Set aside.

❸ GREASE A DEEP 9-inch cake pan or 9-inch springform pan with butter and dust it with flour. Shake out the excess flour. On a lightly floured pastry board, roll out the larger ball of dough (keep the other ball refrigerated) into a 12-inch round. Drape it around the pin and transfer it to the pan. Press it gently onto the bottom and sides of the pan. Prick the bottom lightly with a fork. Brush the egg white lightly over the bottom. Pour in the filling and smooth the top.

❹ ROLL OUT THE remaining dough portion into a round ¼ to ½ inch thick. Using a fluted pastry cutter or sharp knife, cut it into ¾-inch-wide strips. Using the strips, make a lattice-style crust by alternating vertical and horizontal strips to create a woven effect. Cut off any excess pastry, leaving a ½- to 1-inch overhang

to shape into an attractive edge. Pinch the strip ends against the pan rim to form a scalloped effect, as you would when making an apple pie.

❺ IN A SMALL BOWL, beat the egg yolk with the salt and pass it through a small sieve. Brush the edge of the crust and the lattice with the egg yolk wash. Bake on the middle rack of the preheated oven until a cake tester or thin wooden skewer driven through the center of the pie comes out clean and the crust is golden, about 40 minutes. Remove to a rack and let cool until still slightly warm or to room temperature. If using a springform pan, remove the pan sides and transfer the pie to a plate. If using a regular cake pan, serve the pie from the pan. Cut into wedges and serve warm or at room temperature.

AHEAD-OF-TIME NOTE: The dough can be made up to 2 days in advance, tightly wrapped with waxed paper, and refrigerated. Or it can be frozen, wrapped in plastic wrap and aluminum foil, for up to 1 month; to defrost, place in the refrigerator overnight. Once the pie is baked, it will remain fresh for up to a week in the refrigerator and can be reheated in an oven preheated to 350 degrees F for 15 to 20 minutes.

TORTA DI SALSICCIA E FUNGHI

SAUSAGE AND MUSHROOM TART

FOR 8 PEOPLE

❋

THE FLAKY SAVORY TARTS TYPICAL OF GENOESE COOKING ARE THE INSPIRATION FOR THIS LOVELY *torta*. BECAUSE MAKING PUFF PASTRY AT HOME IS TIME-CONSUMING, I HAVE OFTEN FOUND MYSELF RELYING ON THE FROZEN PUFF PASTRY SOLD BY THE POUND IN MANY GOURMET SHOPS AND FRENCH BAKERIES, WHICH CAN BE QUITE GOOD. MAKING IT AT HOME IS VERY SATISFYING, AND THOSE WHO WANT TO LEARN THE METHOD SHOULD READ CAROL FIELD'S EXCELLENT BOOK, *The Italian Baker,* OR MASTER PASTRY CHEF NICHOLAS MALGIERI'S *Great Italian Desserts.* ❋ READY-MADE PUFF PASTRY IS RECTANGULAR IN SHAPE, AND BETWEEN AN EIGHTH AND A QUARTER OF AN INCH THICK. IT MUST BE KEPT CHILLED UNTIL THE MOMENT YOU ARE READY TO USE IT. FILLINGS PLACED ON THE PASTRY SHOULD NOT BE HOT, OR THEY WILL MELT THE BUTTER IN THE PASTRY AND CAUSE HOLES TO FORM. NOTHING MORE NEEDS TO BE DONE THAN TO ROLL IT OUT LIGHTLY TO SMOOTH OUT THE FOLDS. ❋ THE RECIPE FOR THIS FILLING IS FROM A RESTAURATEUR IN BOLOGNA, FRANCO ROSSI, WHO USED IT, COMBINED WITH FRESH POACHED ASPARAGUS, TO FILL *cannelloni* (THE RECIPE IS IN MY BOOK, *Pasta Classica: The Art of Italian Pasta Cooking*). I HAVE FOUND THE SAUSAGE, ONION, MUSHROOM, AND FENNEL COMBINATION SO IRRESISTIBLE, HOWEVER, THAT I USE IT FOR STUFFING MANY THINGS, FROM PASTRY TO PEPPERS (SEE PAGE 28).

FOR THE FILLING:
* ½ *pound fresh white cultivated mushrooms*
* ¼ *cup unsalted butter*
* 1 *small onion, cut into quarters and thinly sliced*
* 1 *teaspoon fennel seed, pulverized in a spice grinder or in a mortar*
* ½ *teaspoon salt*
* *freshly milled black pepper*
* 1 *pound sweet Italian fennel sausages (about 6), casings removed and meat crumbled*

* *approximately 1 pound puff pastry, chilled*
* 1 *egg, lightly beaten with 1 tablespoon milk*
* *olive oil for oiling baking sheet (optional)*

❶ PREHEAT AN OVEN to 425 degrees F. Remove any dirt from the mushrooms with a soft brush or dry cotton towel. Trim off the hard tips of the stems and slice the mushrooms thinly; set aside.

❷ IN A SKILLET over medium-low heat, melt the butter. Add the onion and sauté until softened, 4 to 5 minutes. Add the fennel, salt, pepper to taste, and sausage meat. Sauté until the meat colors but is not hard, 4 to 5 minutes. Add the mushrooms and continue to sauté gently until softened, 3 to 4 minutes. Remove from the heat and allow to cool.

❸ MEANWHILE, place the puff pastry on a lightly floured pastry board and roll it out lightly just to smooth out the creases. Cut it in half horizontally so that you have 2 squares or rectangles (the shape will depend upon the size of the premade pastry). Place the cooled filling in the middle of one of the pastry sheets, leaving a 1-inch border on all sides. Brush the border with some of the egg-milk mixture. Place the second sheet of pastry on top and crimp the edges well all around with a fork to seal. Brush the top with more of the egg-milk mixture.

❹ TRANSFER TO A parchment-lined baking sheet or to a baking sheet that has been lightly greased with oil. Bake in the preheated oven until golden brown, 15 to 20 minutes. Remove to a rack and allow to settle for 5 to 10 minutes. Cut into squares and serve hot or warm.

GRISSINI CON ROSMARINO E SALVIA ALLA PALIO

PALIO'S ROSEMARY AND SAGE BREADSTICKS

MAKES 8 TRAYS, ABOUT 250 BREADSTICKS

ANDREA HELLRIGL, THE TIROLEAN OWNER AND CHEF OF NEW YORK'S ELEGANT PALIO RESTAURANT, GAVE ME THIS RECIPE FOR HIS FAMOUS ROSEMARY AND SAGE BREADSTICKS. THEY ARE RATHER UNUSUAL BECAUSE THE DOUGH IS ROLLED VERY THIN WITH THE AID OF A PASTA MACHINE. I HAVE TRIED ROLLING THEM OUT BY HAND, BUT THEY COME OUT TOO THICK. MR. HELLRIGL SUGGESTS THAT THE DOUGH BE REFRIGERATED OVERNIGHT FOR FLAKIER, CRUNCHIER BREADSTICKS, AND HE ALWAYS USES A ROLLER-TYPE PASTA MACHINE (*not* AN EXTRUSION MACHINE) WITH A *fettuccine* CUTTING ATTACHMENT TO FORM THEM. THE DOUGH IS NOT ALLOWED TO RISE AT ROOM TEMPERATURE, THUS IT REMAINS FIRM AND PASSES EASILY THROUGH THE MACHINE'S ROLLERS AS LONG AS IT IS WELL FLOURED AND COLD. IF A MACHINE IS NOT AVAILABLE, ALLOW THE DOUGH TO COME TO ROOM TEMPERATURE AFTER IT RESTS IN THE REFRIGERATOR OVERNIGHT, AND ROLL IT OUT AS THINLY AS POSSIBLE. BE SURE TO CUT THE DOUGH INTO VERY THIN STICKS (NARROWER THAN A PENCIL) TO ASSURE THAT THEY BAKE CRISPLY.

* *1 cake (20 grams) fresh yeast, or 1 package (scant 1 tablespoon) active dry yeast*
* *2 cups warm water (100 to 110 degrees F)*
* *pinch of sugar*
* *6-¼ cups unbleached all-purpose flour, plus additional flour for working with dough*
* *1 tablespoon salt*
* *¾ teaspoon white pepper*
* *¼ cup extra-virgin olive oil, plus additional olive oil as needed*
* *¼ cup firmly packed, finely chopped mixed fresh rosemary and sage*

❶ IN A SMALL BOWL gently stir the yeast into ¼ cup of the warm water. Add the sugar and let the mixture rest in a warm place for 10 to 15 minutes until it is creamy.

❷ SIFT TOGETHER the 6-¼ cups flour, salt, and pepper into a large bowl and make a well in the center. Add the yeast mixture, the remaining 1-¾ cups water, the ¼ cup oil, and the rosemary and sage to the well. Using a fork, gradually draw the flour into the liquid in the well. When the dough is too stiff to stir with the fork, use your hands to work in the remaining flour. Turn the dough out onto a floured pastry board and knead until smooth, elastic, and not sticky, about 10 minutes. If the dough is still sticky, add a little more flour. Pat the dough into a ball. Oil a clean bowl and place the ball of dough in it. Brush a little oil on the top. Cover the bowl with plastic wrap and refrigerate overnight.

❸ WHEN IT IS TIME to make the breadsticks on the following day, preheat an oven to 350 degrees F. Generously oil 4 baking sheets with olive oil. Take a large handful of dough from the bowl in the refrigerator, leaving the remainder covered and refrigerated, and place it on a lightly floured board. Roll it out as thinly as you can by hand. Dust it with flour and pass it through the rollers of the pasta machine at the first setting (largest opening) to flatten it further. Now fold it in thirds as you would a letter, overlapping the top third and then the bottom third over the middle third. (This will give the dough a uniform shape.) Dust the folded dough lightly with flour and pass it through the first setting again, feeding it from one of its open ends. Now pass the dough through the *fettuccine*-cutting attachment. The *grissini* will be very long–about 1 foot in length–which give them a dramatic effect in a bread basket on the table. Arrange the *grissini* well spaced on a prepared baking sheet. Brush generously with more olive oil. Repeat with the remaining dough, working with a large handful at a time. Fill only as many baking sheets as will fit in your oven comfortably.

❹ BAKE IN THE preheated oven until golden, about 35 minutes. Remove to wire racks to cool. Form and bake the remaining *grissini* in the same manner. Serve them stacked in an oblong bread basket, or standing up in an attractive vessel deep enough to contain them. To store, place them in airtight metal or plastic containers for up to several weeks.

CRESPELLE ALLA DOMENICA MARINO

DOMENICA MARINO'S SAVORY FRITTERS

MAKES ABOUT 25 FRITTERS; FOR 6 PEOPLE

✳

THIS RECIPE WAS SENT TO ME SOME YEARS AGO BY A WOMAN WHOSE GRANDMOTHER, DOMENICA MARINO, HAD EMIGRATED TO AMERICA FROM CALABRIA IN THE EARLY 1900S. SIGNORA MARINO'S COOKING WAS LEGENDARY AMONG FAMILY AND FRIENDS, AND THIS IS ONE OF THE FEW RECIPES THAT WAS WRITTEN DOWN. SHE CALLED THESE FRIED PASTRIES *crespelle* IN DIALECT, ALTHOUGH IN ITALIAN THAT SAME NAME USUALLY REFERS TO THIN BATTER PANCAKES IDENTICAL TO FRENCH *crêpes*. THESE ARE INSTEAD FRITTERS, WHICH GO BY VARIOUS NAMES, INCLUDING *frittelle, ficattole, donzonelline tortucce, arvolte,* AND *crescentini.* ✳ UNLIKE OTHER RECIPES I HAVE SEEN FOR THIS GENRE OF FRIED DOUGH, WHICH ARE GENERALLY BASED ON USING LEFTOVER DOUGH FROM PIZZA OR BREAD, THERE IS NO OIL AND LESS FLOUR IN PROPORTION TO WATER. THESE DETAILS MAKE THIS DOUGH PARTICULARLY LIGHT WHEN FRIED. SIGNORA MARINO STUFFED HER *crespelle* WITH ANCHOVIES, OR SERVED THEM AS A SWEET, DRENCHED IN HONEY OR ROLLED IN SUGAR. DICED *prosciutto, salame, mozzarella,* AND *provolone* ARE ALSO TYPICAL FILLINGS. MY FAVORITE STUFFING IS A MIXTURE OF *soppressata* AND FRESH *mozzarella.* BUT HERE IS A RECIPE WHERE SURELY ONE CANNOT GET INTO TOO MUCH TROUBLE WITH EXPERIMENTATION. USE YOUR IMAGINATION AND TRY OTHER FILLINGS. THE ONLY RULES ARE THAT THEY MUST NOT BE WATERY, AND VEGETABLES, SHRIMP, AND THE LIKE SHOULD BE PRECOOKED.

FOR THE DOUGH:

* ✳ *1 cake (20 grams) fresh yeast, or 1 package (scant 1 tablespoon) active dry yeast*
* ✳ *pinch of sugar*
* ✳ *1-½ cups warm water (100 to 110 degrees F)*
* ✳ *4 cups unbleached all-purpose flour, plus additional flour for working with dough*
* ✳ *1 teaspoon salt*

* ✳ *olive oil for working with dough and for deep-frying*

* ✳ *2 cans (2 ounces each) anchovy fillets in olive oil, drained, or 1/2 pound* salame *and/or* mozzarella, *cut into ½-inch dice*

❶ TO MAKE THE DOUGH, in a small bowl, gently stir the yeast and sugar into the water. Let the mixture rest in a warm place for 15 minutes until it is creamy. Sift the flour onto a large pastry board or kitchen work surface and make a well in the center. Add the yeast mixture and salt to the well. Using a fork or your fingers, gradually draw the flour into the wet ingredients in the well. When the dough becomes too stiff to use a fork, use your hands, wetting them first. Draw in as much flour as is needed to make a soft, pliable, somewhat sticky dough. Generously flour a pastry board or work surface and turn the dough out onto it. Knead the dough until it is lithe and silky, about 10 minutes; it should be softer than pizza dough, even slightly sticky. Use a dough scraper to scrape up any flour that has stuck to the board; put it through a sieve to separate any dried bits of dough from the flour, and then work the flour into the ball of dough.

❷ OIL A LARGE BOWL with olive oil and place the ball of dough in it. Brush a little oil on top and cover with a kitchen towel. Let rise in a warm, draft-free place until doubled, about 1-½ hours.

❸ PUNCH DOWN THE DOUGH, re-cover the bowl, and let rise again until doubled, about 1 hour. Punch it down again and knead for several minutes to return it to a silky, elastic, and slightly sticky consistency. Cover the bowl with a damp towel to prevent the dough from forming a crust.

❹ IF USING ANCHOVIES, pat them with a paper towel to rid them of their oil. Cut them in half crosswise. If using *salame* and/or *mozzarella*, place in a small bowl on your work surface.

❺ DIVIDE THE DOUGH into quarters. Work with only one quarter at a time, always re-covering the bowl with the damp towel until ready for more dough. Oil both hands lightly because the dough will be slightly sticky. Pull off about 1 tablespoon of the dough from the quarter portion and press a piece of anchovy into the center of it, or a little of the *salame* and/or *mozzarella*. Pinch the dough closed over the filling, seal firmly to close, and stretch the dough to a length of about 4 inches (the dough will spring back, but this stretching will make the fritters lighter when they are fried). As the fritters are formed, transfer them to floured baking sheets. When all of the fritters are made, cover with dry cotton towels and allow to rise until doubled, about 45 minutes.

❻ PREHEAT AN OVEN to 200 degrees F. Pour olive oil into a deep skillet to a depth of 1 inch and heat to 375 degrees F, or until a small piece of dough sizzles instantly when dropped into it. Drop 4 or 5 fritters into the sizzling hot oil, making sure there is enough room between them to allow them to expand. Cook until golden on all sides, about 6 minutes. Lift out the fritters with a slotted utensil and transfer them to a pan lined with paper towels to drain. Repeat with the remaining fritters, oiling your hands again if the fritters begin sticking to them as you pick them up off the baking sheets. Place the cooked, drained fritters in the warm oven until all the fritters are cooked. Eat piping hot.

NOTE: The fritters can be fried in advance and kept for up to a week in the refrigerator. Reheat in an oven preheated to 350 degrees F until very hot, 15 to 20 minutes.

CROSTATA DI CIPOLLE VERDI ALL'AMENDOLARA

ANNA AMENDOLARA'S GREEN ONION PIE

FOR 8 PEOPLE

❋

THIS WONDERFUL RUSTIC PIE, INVENTED BY ANNA AMENDOLARA NURSE, HAS ITS ROOTS IN THE BARESE (FROM BARI, IN APULIA) COOKING SHE GREW UP WITH AND DOES SO WELL. SHE THREW IT TOGETHER QUICKLY ONE AFTERNOON, SHE TOLD ME, WHEN SHE WAS EXPECTING HER FAMOUS FRIEND, AFRICAN-AMERICAN COOK, CHEF, AND COOKBOOK AUTHOR EDNA LEWIS, FOR LUNCH. EDNA LOVED IT, AND SO DO I. THE FEW INGREDIENTS ARE SMASHING TOGETHER. IF YOU CAN BUY ANCHOVIES BOTTLED IN HOT-PEPPER OIL, USE THEM IN THE FILLING. OTHERWISE, ADD HOT-PEPPER FLAKES TO TASTE WHEN SAUTÉING THE ONIONS.

❋ *crust recipe for Emilian Spinach Pie (page 119)*

FOR THE FILLING:
❋ *⅓ cup extra-virgin olive oil*
❋ *¼ teaspoon dried red-pepper flakes, or to taste*
❋ *12 bunches green onions, white part and 1 inch of green, cut into 1-inch lengths*
❋ *1 cup pitted and sliced, sharp-flavored green olives*
❋ *1 can (2 ounces) anchovy fillets in olive oil, drained and cut into small pieces*

❋ *1 egg, beaten with 1 drop water for the crust*

❶ MAKE THE PASTRY DOUGH for the crust as directed and chill. Preheat an oven to 400 degrees F.

❷ TO MAKE THE FILLING, in a large skillet over high heat, warm the olive oil. When hot enough to make the onions sizzle, add some of the pepper flakes and one third to one half of the onions, and sauté until nicely seared, about 5 minutes. It is best to cook the onions in 2 or 3 batches, removing them with a slotted spoon to allow the oil to remain in the pan; otherwise, they will stew rather than sear evenly. When all the onions are sautéed, transfer them to a colander placed over a bowl and allow the oil to drain off while they cool. Reserve the nicely flavored oil for another purpose.

❸ MEANWHILE, roll out the dough and line the pan as directed in the spinach pie recipe. In a bowl toss together the onions, olives, and anchovies and fill the pie shell with the mix-

ture. Roll out the remaining pastry and top the pie as directed in the spinach pie. Cut a slash in the top to allow steam to escape.

❹ BRUSH THE CRUST with the beaten egg and bake until golden, about 30 minutes. Remove from the oven and cool on a rack for 15 minutes. Serve hot or warm, cut into wedges.

NOTE: This pie keeps well in the refrigerator for up to 3 days. Reheat it in an oven preheated to 300 degrees F until warm throughout, 20 to 30 minutes.

LEFT: Scarpazzone al Forno (page 119)

PIZZA ALLA NAPOLETANA

CLASSIC NEAPOLITAN PIZZA

MAKES ONE 14-BY-16-INCH PIZZA, TWO 12-INCH ROUND PIZZAS, OR FOUR 6-INCH ROUND PIZZAS; FOR 8 TO 12 PEOPLE

I DO NOT OFFER THIS RECIPE FOR ITS NOVELTY, FOR IN AMERICA A FACSIMILE OF IT IS CERTAINLY THE MOST FAMILIAR OF THE PIZZA TRIBE. BUT A PERFECTLY PRODUCED PIZZA NEAPOLITAN STYLE, AS SIMPLE AS IT IS TO MAKE, IS A RARE FIND HERE. THE TOPPING IS UNCOMPLICATED, CONSISTING OF LITTLE MORE THAN CHOPPED UNCOOKED TOMATOES, FRUITY OLIVE OIL, GARLIC, AND A SCATTERING OF OREGANO. CHEESE LOVERS CAN ADD SHREDDED *mozzarella*, ALTHOUGH THE CLASSIC NEAPOLITAN PIZZA CONTAINS NONE. THE DOUGH IS A BASIC ONE FROM WHICH ALL *pizze, crespelle, pizzelle, calzoncelli* (MINIATURE BAKED STUFFED PIZZAS), AND OTHER SUCH SAVORY BREADS CAN BE MADE.

FOR THE DOUGH:

* ✳ *½ cake (10 grams) fresh yeast, or 1-¼ teaspoons active dry yeast*
* ✳ *⅛ teaspoon sugar*
* ✳ *1-¼ cups warm water (100 to 110 degrees F)*
* ✳ *about 4 cups unbleached all-purpose flour*
* ✳ *1-¼ teaspoons salt*
* ✳ *3 tablespoons extra-virgin olive oil, plus additional olive oil as needed*
* ✳ *cornmeal for baker's peel, if using*

FOR THE TOPPING:

* ✳ *3 cups well-drained, peeled, seeded, and chopped fresh or canned tomatoes*
* ✳ *6 large cloves garlic, peeled and coarsely chopped*
* ✳ *2 tablespoons chopped fresh oregano, or 1 tablespoon dried oregano*
* ✳ *6 tablespoons extra-virgin olive oil*
* ✳ *salt*

✳ ✳ ✳

❶ TO MAKE THE DOUGH, in a small bowl gently stir the yeast and sugar into ¼ cup of the water. Let the mixture rest in a warm place for 10 to 15 minutes until it is creamy.

❷ SIFT TOGETHER 1 cup of the flour and the salt into a large, shallow bowl and make a well in the center. Add the 3 tablespoons olive oil and the remaining 1 cup water to the yeast mixture and pour the liquid into the well. Using a wooden spoon, gradually stir the flour into the liquid until it is absorbed. With the spoon, gradually work in 2 more cups flour, sifting it as you add it. When the dough becomes too stiff to stir with the spoon, use your hands to incorporate the flour.

❸ FLOUR A PASTRY BOARD or work surface well with some of the remaining flour and turn the dough out onto it. Shape the dough into a ball, then begin kneading the dough while gradually sifting onto it as much of the remaining flour as needed to form a dough that is neither sticky nor too hard. Now knead the dough until it is smooth and elastic; 8 to 10 minutes.

❹ LIGHTLY OIL another large mixing bowl and place the ball of dough in it. Lightly brush the surface of the dough with oil. Cover the bowl tightly with plastic wrap. Let rise in a warm, draft-free place until doubled, 1 to 1-½ hours.

❺ IF USING A PIZZA PAN, preheat an oven to 400 degrees F. If using a baking stone or terracotta tiles, place in the oven and preheat to 450 degrees F for 40 minutes.

❻ WHILE THE OVEN is preheating, punch down the dough, turn it out onto a lightly floured board, and knead it for several minutes until it is once again elastic. (If you wish to make more than one pizza, divide the dough into portions as desired at this point.) Roll the dough out to make a ¼- to ½-inch-thick pizza base. Turn the dough disk over several times as you roll to prevent it from shrinking back. Transfer the disk to an oiled pizza pan. Using your fingers, shape the disk to fit the contours of the pan. Then use your fingers to push the dough toward the rim in order to create an edge that is about twice as thick as the center of the pie. If you are using a baker's peel, form the edge while the disk is on the board, then transfer it to the peel sprinkled with cornmeal. (If you have a baking stone or tiles but no peel, transfer the pizza base to a cornmeal-dusted baking sheet without sides.)

❼ COVER THE PIZZA BASE with a cotton kitchen towel and let rise in a warm place undisturbed for 30 minutes.

❽ FOR THE TOPPING, first place the tomatoes in a colander and press down on them with a wooden spoon to drain excess juices. Place them in a bowl, add the garlic and oregano, and mix well. Distribute with the tomato mixture over the pizza, drizzle the olive oil, and brush the edges of the crust as well. Sprinkle to taste with salt.

❾ IF USING A PIZZA PAN, bake the pie in the preheated oven until edges are golden, about 20 minutes. If using a baking stone or tiles, slide the pizza off the peel (or the baking sheet) directly onto the heated surface. Bake until the edges are golden, 15 to 20 minutes. Use a pastry wheel to cut the pizza into wedges. Serve hot.

SCARPAZZONE AL FORNO

EMILIAN SPINACH PIE

FOR 6 TO 8 PEOPLE

✸

IN EMILIA THIS PIE IS CALLED *scarpazzone* or *erbazzone*, REFERRING TO ITS FILLING OF *erbe*, "GREENS," WHICH CAN BE EITHER SPINACH OR SWISS CHARD. THE *pancetta* PAIRS IRRESISTIBLY WITH THE MILDLY GARLICKY GREENS, AND THE BEATEN EGG BINDS THE FILLING. THE FLAKY CRUST IS SIMILAR TO AN AMERICAN PIE CRUST.

FOR THE CRUST:
* ✸ *2-½ cups unbleached all-purpose flour, plus additional flour for working with dough*
* ✸ *1 teaspoon salt*
* ✸ *⅔ cup unsalted butter, lard, or vegetable shortening, chilled*
* ✸ *½ cup ice water*

FOR THE FILLING:
* ✸ *1 pound spinach or Swiss chard, stemmed*
* ✸ *2 tablespoons unsalted butter*
* ✸ *2 ounces* pancetta *or bacon, chopped*
* ✸ *1 small onion, chopped*
* ✸ *1 clove garlic, finely chopped*
* ✸ *1 tablespoon chopped fresh Italian parsley*
* ✸ *1 tablespoon fine dried bread crumbs*
* ✸ *¼ cup freshly grated* parmigiano
* ✸ *1 egg, beaten*
* ✸ *½ teaspoon salt*
* ✸ *freshly milled black pepper*

* ✸ *1 egg, beaten*

❶ TO MAKE THE PIE CRUST, stir together the flour and salt in a mixing bowl. Using a pastry blender or 2 knives, cut in the butter, lard, or shortening until pea-sized pieces form. Using a fork, mix in the ice water, a little at a time, until it is evenly distributed. Gather the mixture into a ball, trying to handle it as little as possible. Wrap it tightly in plastic wrap and refrigerate for 30 minutes.

❷ MEANWHILE, preheat an oven to 350 degrees F. To make the filling, place the spinach or chard in a saucepan without the addition of any more water than the drops still clinging to the leaves from washing. Cover and cook over medium heat until tender, just a few minutes. Remove from the heat, let cool, then using your hands, squeeze out as much water as you can. Chop finely and set aside.

❸ IN A SKILLET over medium heat, melt the butter. Add the *pancetta* or bacon and sauté until browned, about 3 minutes. Add the onion, garlic, and parsley and sauté gently until soft, about 4 minutes; do not brown. Add the chopped spinach or chard and mix well. Remove from the heat and add the bread crumbs, cheese, egg, salt, and pepper to taste. Set aside.

❹ DIVIDE THE DOUGH into 2 portions, one slightly larger than the other. On a lightly floured board roll out the larger portion into an 11-inch round. Drape it around the pin and transfer it to a deep 9-inch pie pan. Press it gently onto the bottom and sides of the pan. Spoon in the filling. Roll out the second ball of dough in the same manner into a slightly smaller circle. Lay it over the filling. Crimp the edges together to seal and trim off any excess to form an even edge. Cut a slash in the top to allow steam to escape. If there are any dough scraps, gather them up, reroll them, and cut out leaves or rosettes. Decorate the top of the pie with the cutouts, pressing them gently onto the crust.

❺ BRUSH THE CRUST with the beaten egg and bake in the preheated oven until golden, about 35 minutes. Remove from the oven and transfer it to a rack to cool for about 10 minutes. Serve hot or warm, cut into wedges.

NOTE: This pie keeps well in the refrigerator for up to 3 days. Reheat it in an oven preheated to 300 degrees F until warm throughout, 20 to 30 minutes.

TRAMEZZINI

MINIATURE TRIANGULAR SANDWICHES WITH VARIOUS FILLINGS

FOR 6 PEOPLE

THESE ARE THE SMALL, ELEGANT SANDWICHES TO BE ACCOMPANIED WITH APERITIFS THAT ONE SEES PILED UP ON BAR COUNTERS IN ITALY. THEY MAKE LOVELY *antipasti* OR PARTY FOOD. FOR THE BASES, USE SQUARE SLICES OF WHITE BREAD, CRUSTS REMOVED AND SPREAD GENEROUSLY WITH THE BUTTER MIXTURE BELOW. THE FILLINGS ARE UP TO ANYONE'S *fantasia*—"IMAGINATION"—BUT SOME CLASSIC ITALIAN COMBINATIONS FOLLOW. OR YOU MIGHT CHOOSE TO FILL THEM WITH ANY OF THE FLAVORED BUTTERS ON PAGE 132. ONCE THE SANDWICHES ARE FILLED, THEY ARE CUT INTO QUARTERS ON THE DIAGONAL SO THAT FOUR LITTLE TRIANGLES RESULT. THE *tramezzini* ARE EASIER TO CUT AND TO BITE INTO IF MEAT, CHEESE, AND SUCH ARE SLICED AS THINLY AS POSSIBLE. THE SANDWICHES LOOK NEAT AND DELICATE IF THE FILLINGS ARE CUT TO FIT WITHIN THE SQUARES EXACTLY OR TRIMMED TO PREVENT OVERHANG. ❀ TO KEEP THE *tramezzini* MOIST UNTIL SERVING, LINE A PLATTER WITH A COTTON DISH TOWEL THAT HAS BEEN SOAKED IN WATER AND WRUNG OUT THOROUGHLY. PLACE THE SANDWICHES ON THE PLATE AND THEN BRING THE FOUR CORNERS OF THE TOWEL TOGETHER TO COVER THEM THOROUGHLY. IF YOU ARE PREPARING THE SANDWICHES IN ADVANCE, WRAP THE TOWEL-COVERED PLATE TIGHTLY WITH PLASTIC WRAP AS WELL AND REFRIGERATE.

---

* *½ cup (¼ pound) unsalted butter, at room temperature*
* *1 teaspoon water*
* *1 teaspoon Dijon-style mustard*
* *½ loaf (about ½ pound) good white bread, very thinly sliced and crusts removed*

IN A BLENDER OR FOOD PROCESSOR, combine the butter, water, and mustard and whip until well blended, light, and fluffy. Spread the whipped butter onto the bread slices and fill with one of the following suggested fillings.

Tramezzini with frittata: Prepare any *frittata* (chapter 3), cooking it in a large skillet in order to make it very thin. Allow it to cool. Butter the bread slices with the butter spread and fill them with squares of *frittata*. Cut each sandwich on the diagonal into quarters.

Tramezzini with chicken breasts: Divide 1 boned whole chicken breast in half and place the halves between sheets of waxed paper. Using a meat mallet or the dull side of a cleaver blade, pound the breasts as thinly as possible to flatten without tearing them. Sauté the pounded breasts in 3 tablespoons unsalted butter with a few fresh sage leaves or ¼ teaspoon dried sage for about 3 minutes on each side. Add salt and freshly milled black pepper to taste and remove from the pan. Deglaze the pan with ¼ cup dry white wine. Return the breasts to the pan to coat them with the wine. Allow to cool. Cut the breasts to fit between the bread squares. Butter the bread slices with the butter spread and place chicken pieces on half of them. Top with slices of ham cut to fit within the bread slices. Top each with another bread slice. Cut each sandwich on the diagonal into quarters.

Tramezzini with prosciutto and fontina: Butter bread slices with the butter spread or with Anchovy Butter (page xx). Place thin slices of *prosciutto* and *fontina* cheese on half of the slices. Top each with another bread slice. Cut each sandwich on the diagonal into quarters.

Tramezzini with salame: Butter bread slices with the butter spread. Place slices of good-quality *soppressata* or other *salame* between the slices. Cut each sandwich on the diagonal into quarters.

Tramezzini with mozzarella: Butter slices of bread with the butter spread. Place thin slices of fresh *mozzarella* and fresh sweet tomatoes on half of the slices. Top each with another bread slice. Cut each sandwich on the diagonal into quarters.

Tramezzini all'arlecchino: Butter bread slices with the butter spread or with Light Lemon Mayonnaise (page 127). Place thin slices of freshly roasted chicken and sweet tomatoes, soft lettuce, *fontina* cheese, and sliced hard-cooked eggs on half the slices. Top each with another bread slice. Cut each sandwich on the diagonal into quarters.

FARINATA

SAVORY LIGURIAN CHICK-PEA FLAT BREAD

FOR 6 PEOPLE

❋

ONE FINDS THIS SPECIALTY IN THE NORTHWEST COASTAL REGION FROM LIVORNO IN NORTH TUSCANY TO NICE AND MARSEILLES IN PROVENCE. WHILE *farinata* IS MOST OFTEN PREPARED IN LOCAL BAKERIES, WHERE CUSTOMERS LINE UP WAITING FOR IT TO EMERGE PIPING HOT FROM ENORMOUS WOOD-BURNING OVENS, IT CAN BE MADE AT HOME IN A VERY HOT OVEN IF A HEAVY, SEASONED CAST-IRON OR OVENPROOF NONSTICK SKILLET IS AVAILABLE. MADE FROM NOTHING MORE THAN CHICK-PEA FLOUR, WATER, AND OIL (ONIONS AND OLIVES ARE SOMETIMES ADDED), IT IS ALMOST PURE PROTEIN.

* *3 cups chick-pea flour*
* *4-⅓ cups water*
* *½ teaspoon salt*
* *plenty of freshly milled black pepper*
* *2 tablespoons extra-virgin olive oil, plus additional olive oil as needed*
* *1 small red onion, halved and thinly sliced*
* *⅓ cup pitted and sliced, good-quality Italian or French black olives such as Gaeta or Niçoise*

❶ COMBINE THE CHICK-PEA flour and water in a bowl and let rest at room temperature for at least 1 hour or for up to 12 hours.

❷ PREHEAT AN OVEN to 500 degrees F. Skim off and discard the foam from the top of the batter. Stir in the salt, pepper, 2 tablespoons olive oil, onion, and olives. Generously oil a 12-inch nonstick, ovenproof skillet with olive oil. Pour in only enough of the batter to form a layer no more than ⅛ inch thick. Place on the top rack in the preheated oven and bake until browned on top, about 20 minutes. Remove, cut into wedges, and eat immediately. Bake one batch at a time in order to serve the *farinata* hot.

CROSTINI

TOASTS

MAKES ABOUT 60 PIECES

Crostini ARE SIMPLY TOASTS UPON WHICH THE ITALIANS SPREAD ANY NUMBER OF SAVORY TOPPINGS. BUT NOT JUST ANY BREAD WILL DO. BREAD FOR *crostini* SHOULD HAVE A FIRM TEXTURE AND A GOOD CRUST; IT SHOULD NOT BE LIGHT AND AIRY. BUY GOOD-QUALITY, SUBSTANTIAL ITALIAN LOAVES OR FRENCH BAGUETTES THAT WILL ACCEPT MOIST OR JUICY TOPPINGS WITHOUT DISINTEGRATING. THE NUMBER OF *crostini* YOU END UP WITH DEPENDS UPON THE LENGTH OF THE LOAVES. *Crostini* CAN BE FRIED, BAKED IN THE OVEN, OR TOASTED LIGHTLY ON A GRILL, IF YOU HAVE ONE GOING. TOP THEM WITH THE CHICKEN LIVER SPREAD ON PAGE 67, OR WITH ANY OF THE SPREADS OR COMPOSED BUTTERS IN CHAPTER 8.

✳ *1 loaf substantial Italian or French bread, 2 to 3 inches in diameter*
✳ *extra-virgin olive oil or unsalted butter, at room temperature, as needed*

❶ Cut the bread into ¼-inch-thick slices. To fry them, in a large skillet over medium-low heat, pour in enough olive oil or melt enough butter to cover generously the bottom surface of the bread slices once they are added. When the oil or butter is hot enough to make the bread sizzle, arrange as many bread slices in the pan as you can without crowding. Fry the slices on both sides, turning once. Add more oil or butter for the next batch.

❷ TO BAKE THE *crostini,* preheat an oven to 400 degrees F. Brush the bread slices on both sides with olive oil or butter and place them on a baking sheet. Bake until golden on both sides, turning once, 12 to 15 minutes' total cooking time.

❸ TO GRILL THE *crostini,* prepare a charcoal fire in an outdoor grill or preheat an indoor grill. Brush the bread slices on both sides with olive oil or butter and place them on the grill as far as possible from the heat source. Grill until golden on both sides. The length of time will vary depending upon the type of grill you use, but the *crostini* will burn quickly on the grill, so stand over them with tongs and be prepared to turn them quickly as they toast.

THE *crostini* can be eaten hot or at room temperature. Store them in airtight containers for up to 2 weeks.

Chapter 8

SAUCES &
SPREADS

• • •

Salsa e burri composti

GENERALLY sauces are not as sophisticated or as important in

the Italian kitchen as they are in French cuisine. When my Italian relations travel to France, I sometimes ask them how they liked the food. On more than one occasion they have wrinkled up their noses and replied, "We couldn't tell. There were too many sauces on it." At the root of this response is the Italian preference for an earthy, peasant-based cooking style in which food is prepared with the purpose of keeping the flavors and identity of the ingredients intact. Instead of combining many different flavors to achieve a new taste experience, or masking food with artful sauces, the Italian approach is to use fresh, quality ingredients and to cook them simply in order to bring out their natural flavors. ❈ The gastronomical battle between the Italians and the French goes back to when Caterina de' Medici married Henry II in 1533 and transported her Florentine kitchen to France. Her cooks created a veritable culinary renaissance there with their sauces, spices, and devotion to food, influencing French tables forever. But in subsequent centuries, Italy's economy declined and its "court cuisine" was mostly lost. Ever since, however, the two nations have fought over whose food is better and whose culinary triumphs originated where. The question of sauces is a particularly sticky one, since they originated with the Italians but became highly evolved with the French. Italian sauces are rarely based on cream or stock, as the French are, but rely on olive oil, wine, and herbs for flavoring, and bread crumbs, cheese, or chopped vegetables *(odori)* for body. In the south of Italy, tomatoes are predominant where sauces are found, but not to the extent that Americans are used to from their experience of hybrid American-Italian food. ❈ The most familiar Italian sauces

127	132
MAIONESE LEGGERA AL LIMONE	**BURRI COMPOSTI**
light lemon mayonnaise	flavored butters
MAIONESE VERDE	BURRO DI TONNO
green mayonnaise	tuna butter
MAIONESE CON AGLIO	BURRO DI GORGONZOLA
garlic mayonnaise	*gorgonzola* butter
128	BURRO DI CAVIALE
PEPERONATA	caviar butter
roasted red and yellow pepper spread	BURRO DI SALMONE AFFUMICATO
129	smoked salmon butter
SALMORIGLIO	BURRO D'ACCIUGA
Sicilian lemon sauce	anchovy butter
129	133
POMAROLA ("PUMMAROLA")	**SALSA VERDE**
Neapolitan-style tomato sauce	green sauce
130	134
PURÉ DI OLIVE	**SALSA DI POMODORO AL BASILICO**
olive purée	sieved tomato sauce with basil
130	135
PÂTÉ DI MELANZANA	**SALSA ROSSA CRUDA**
eggplant spread	uncooked tomato sauce

are perhaps *béchamel* (about which the Italians and the French are in a deadlock as to which of their nations invented it) and fresh mayonnaise. *Béchamel* is discussed at length and a recipe appears in my book, *Pasta Classica: The Art of Italian Pasta Cooking.* Both of these sauces have varied uses as anointments and as bindings in *antipasti* dishes. Light, quickly cooked tomato sauces are also useful on the *antipasto* table, especially with stuffed vegetables and for topping *pizzelle* (little pizzas). The uncooked tomato salsa and spreads that are included in this chapter are delicious on *crostini,* and have many other uses on the antipasto table. *Salsa verde,* a simple, heady mixture of extra-virgin olive oil, lemon, parsley, capers, and chopped cornichons, is for poached fish or meat, and many *antipasti* dishes in this category benefit from it. *Bagnet* is a Piedmontese parsley sauce much like *salsa verde,* but without the cornichons, and also containing chopped anchovy and mustard (see the dressing for the grilled beef salad in chapter 4). *Salmoriglio,* a silky Sicilian sauce made from blending good olive oil with lemon juice and oregano or other herbs, gives zest to fish and vegetable *antipasti.* ❀ The *burri composti,* or "composed butters," in this chapter are useful on *crostini* of all kinds, from bread to *polenta,* and for *tramezzini,* the dainty little sandwiches described in chapter 7. They can also be blended with the yolks of hard-cooked eggs for filling stuffed eggs. ❀ ❀ ❀

MAIONESE LEGGERA AL LIMONE

LIGHT LEMON MAYONNAISE

MAKES ABOUT 1 CUP

✻

MAYONNAISE, LIKE BREAD AND FRESH EGG PASTA (NOT TO BE CONFUSED WITH FACTORY-PRODUCED DRIED PASTA, WHICH IS A MARVELOUS PRODUCT) HAS TO BE FRESHLY MADE TO BE GOOD. COMMERCIALLY PRODUCED MAYONNAISES CONTAIN ALL MANNER OF STRANGE INGREDIENTS, NOT TO MENTION SUGAR. SUCH SWEET MAYONNAISES WILL NOT DO IN ITALIAN COOKING. MAKING MAYONNAISE AT HOME IS QUITE SIMPLE, AND I OFFER THE SIMPLEST METHOD HERE. ✻ IT IS IMPORTANT THAT THE UTENSILS YOU USE ARE WARM AND THAT ALL THE INGREDIENTS ARE AT ROOM TEMPERATURE, THAT IS, OUT OF THE REFRIGERATOR FOR AN HOUR OR MORE. I HAVE ALWAYS WATCHED MY ITALIAN RELATIVES WHIP UP FRESH MAYONNAISE IN MINUTES BY HAND, USING NOTHING MORE THAN A WOODEN SPOON FOR BEATING THE OIL INTO THE EGG. I PREFER TO MAKE IT IN A BLENDER, HOWEVER. IT GOES QUICKLY THIS WAY, EVEN FOR THE NOVICE. WHILE CLASSIC RECIPES FOR *maionese* CALL FOR TWO EGG YOLKS FOR THIS QUANTITY OF OIL, I LIKE TO USE A WHOLE EGG INSTEAD. IT MAKES THE MAYONNAISE LIGHTER AND MORE NUTRITIOUS (EGG WHITE IS PURE PROTEIN, WHILE THE YOLKS ARE COMPRISED MOSTLY OF FAT). ✻ LOVELY *antipasti* ARE MADE BY DRIZZLING THIS LIGHT, SILKY MAYONNAISE ON FRESHLY BOILED ARTICHOKE HEARTS, STEAMED LOBSTER, OR WARM BOILED POTATOES, JUST TO NAME A FEW POSSIBILITIES.

✻ ½ cup safflower oil or vegetable oil
✻ ¼ cup extra-virgin olive oil
✻ 1 egg, at room temperature
✻ ½ teaspoon salt, or to taste
✻ 2 tablespoons freshly squeezed lemon juice, or to taste
✻ ½ teaspoon Dijon-style mustard
✻ dash of freshly milled white pepper

❶ COMBINE THE OILS in a small pitcher. Crack the egg into the jar of a blender and blend briefly to beat lightly. Add 2 tablespoons of the oils. Blend on high speed for 10 seconds. With the machine on the same setting, add the remaining oil in a very thin, slow, steady stream. It is crucial not to add too much oil at once or the mayonnaise will not emulsify. Turn off the blender motor. Use a rubber spatula to scrape the inside of the blender jar so that all the ingredients are thoroughly combined. Stir the salt into the lemon juice and add it with the mustard and pepper. Engage the blender again to combine thoroughly. Use immediately or cover and chill. Homemade mayonnaise will keep for a week in the refrigerator.

MAIONESE VERDE
Green Mayonnaise
To 1 CUP MAYONNAISE, add 2 tablespoons finely chopped fresh Italian parsley; 2 tablespoons finely chopped cornichons; 1 tablespoon chopped drained capers; 1 tablespoon freshly squeezed lemon juice, or to taste; freshly milled black pepper to taste; and half a small anchovy fillet, well mashed, or ½ teaspoon anchovy paste. Mix together all the ingredients, blending with a wooden spoon. Serve with sliced boiled meats and chicken, or on hard-cooked eggs.

MAIONESE CON AGLIO
Garlic Mayonnaise
To 1 CUP MAYONNAISE, add 2 large cloves garlic, finely chopped or passed through a garlic press and then pounded into a paste with a little salt. Serve with seafood, especially steamed lobster or shellfish.

PEPERONATA

ROASTED RED AND YELLOW PEPPER SPREAD

FOR 4 TO 6 PEOPLE

✳

THIS IS AN ADAPTATION OF A DELICIOUS SPREAD SERVED TO ME BY KAREN FORHALTZ AND MICHAEL MIELE, TWO ITALOPHILES WHO, WHEN NOT RUNNING AMSTERDAM'S IN MANHATTAN, ARE ALWAYS OFF EXPLORING ITALY IN SEARCH OF ITS GASTRONOMIC TREASURES. IT IS PERFECT SERVED ON *crostini,* THE THINLY SLICED ROUNDS OF TOASTED ITALIAN OR FRENCH BREAD FOR WHICH A RECIPE IS GIVEN ON PAGE 123. THERE ARE MANY VERSIONS OF *peperonata.* SOME CONTAIN ONION, SOME CONTAIN OLIVES OR CAPERS, AND SOME INCLUDE TOMATOES, AMONG OTHER THINGS. BUT THIS SIMPLE TRIO OF ROASTED SWEET PEPPERS, FRUITY EXTRA-VIRGIN OLIVE OIL, AND A LITTLE GARLIC HAS SO MUCH FLAVOR THAT THE ADDITION OF ANYTHING ELSE WOULD MUDDLE RATHER THAN ENHANCE. IN FACT, LITTLE IF ANY SALT AND PEPPER ARE NECESSARY.

✳ *2 yellow bell peppers*
✳ *2 red bell peppers*
✳ *½ cup extra-virgin olive oil*
✳ *1 large garlic clove, finely chopped or passed through a garlic press*
✳ *salt and freshly milled black pepper*
✳ *1 recipe Toasts (page 123)*

❶ ROAST THE BELL PEPPERS as directed on page 28, then peel, halve, stem, seed, and derib. Place on a cutting board and chop finely with a knife or *mezzaluna* ("half-moon") chopper. Do not use a food processor, which will purée rather than chop, causing the brilliant red and yellow colors of the peppers to blend rather than to retain their separate identities. Transfer to a serving bowl and add the oil, garlic, and salt and pepper to taste. Mix well. Serve with the *crostini.*

SALMORIGLIO

SICILIAN LEMON SAUCE

MAKES ABOUT ⅔ CUP

❋

THIS TANGY SAUCE HAS MANY USES ON THE *antipasto* TABLE. DRIZZLE IT OVER SKEWERED GRILLED OR BROILED SCALLOPS OR SHRIMP, OR OVER BROILED OR GRILLED SWORDFISH OR TUNA KABOBS. STEAMED OR BOILED VEGETABLES SUCH AS GREEN BEANS OR SLICED COOKED BEETS ARE TRANSFORMED INSTANTLY INTO TASTY *antipasti* WHEN THEY ARE DRESSED WITH *salmoriglio*.

❋ *2 tablespoons freshly squeezed lemon juice*
❋ *¼ cup extra-virgin olive oil*
❋ *2 small cloves garlic, finely chopped or*
   passed through a garlic press
❋ *1 teaspoon chopped fresh oregano, or*
   ½ teaspoon dried oregano

❶ PUT THE LEMON JUICE into a small bowl. Add the olive oil to it in a slow, steady stream, using a whisk or electric beater to beat the sauce into an emulsion. Add the garlic, continuing to beat. Stir in the oregano. Cover and store in the refrigerator for 1 to 2 weeks or longer.

POMAROLA ("PUMMAROLA")

NEAPOLITAN-STYLE TOMATO SAUCE

MAKES ABOUT 2-½ CUPS

❋

BECAUSE OF THE PRESENCE OF UNSIEVED VEGETABLES, THIS CHUNKY SAUCE HAS GOOD BODY AND A LOT OF FLAVOR. I MIX IT WITH *risotto* FOR MAKING CROQUETTES (SEE PAGE 40), AND IT IS A GOOD, FAST, ALL-PURPOSE SAUCE FOR TOPPING PIZZA AND *pizzelle* AND FOR PASTA.

❋ *2-½ pounds fresh vine-ripened tomatoes (2-½ cups),*
   or 1 can (28 ounces) plum tomatoes in purée,
   seeded and finely chopped
❋ *3 tablespoons extra-virgin olive oil*
❋ *1 small onion, finely chopped*
❋ *2 celery stalks, finely chopped*
❋ *1 large carrot, peeled and finely chopped*
❋ *1 tablespoon chopped fresh basil*
❋ *salt and freshly milled black pepper*

❶ IF USING FRESH TOMATOES, bring a large saucepan filled with water to a boil. Add the tomatoes, blanch for 30 seconds, drain, and immediately plunge them into cold water. Remove the skins and seeds and finely chop.
❷ IN A SAUCEPAN over medium heat, warm the oil. Add the onion, celery, and carrots, and sauté until the vegetables are soft, about 10 minutes. Press them with the back of a wooden spoon to release their flavors. Add the tomatoes and simmer, partially covered, 20 minutes for fresh tomatoes and 35 minutes for canned tomatoes. Add the basil and season to taste with salt and pepper.

AHEAD-OF-TIME NOTE: This sauce can be made up to 4 days in advance, covered, and refrigerated.

PURÉ DI OLIVE

OLIVE PURÉE

FOR 4 TO 6 PEOPLE

❉

YOU MUST USE THE BEST OLIVES AND OLIVE OIL FOR MAKING THIS OLIVE PASTE, WHICH IS GOOD ON *crostini* (PAGE 123), OR EVEN AS A SAUCE FOR *spaghetti*. THE OLIVES SHOULD BE FULL, FLESHY, IMPORTED ITALIAN OR FRENCH BLACK OLIVES SUCH AS NIÇOISE OR GAETA OLIVES (GREEK KALAMATA ARE TOO SOUR). BE VERY SURE THAT THE OLIVES HAVE NOT BEEN SUSPENDED IN WATER OR PRESERVED IN A TOO SOUR-TASTING, VINEGARY BRINE. RAW (UNCOOKED) EXTRA-VIRGIN OLIVE OIL HAS FRAGRANCE AND FLAVOR THAT ARE PARTIALLY LOST IN COOKING. IN THIS RECIPE, THAT FLAVOR IS FULLY EXPERIENCED. DO NOT USE A FOOD PROCESSOR OR BLENDER TO CHOP ANY OF THE INGREDIENTS. THEY MUST BE CHOPPED WITH A KNIFE OR *mezzaluna* CHOPPER TO ACHIEVE THE PROPER TEXTURE.

❉ *½ pound black olives*
❉ *1 large clove garlic, finely chopped or passed through a garlic press*
❉ *½ teaspoon chopped fresh marjoram, or ¼ teaspoon dried marjoram*
❉ *¼ cup extra-virgin olive oil*

❶ CUT THE OLIVE FLESH off the pits. You should have about 1 cup. Chop coarsely. In a bowl combine the olives, garlic, and marjoram. Mix with a wooden spoon. Add the olive oil, a little at a time, blending the mixture with the spoon as you do. Be careful not to mash the olives.

AHEAD-OF-TIME NOTE: This purée will last for a few weeks in the refrigerator if you cover it with olive oil, but bring it to room temperature before using it.

PÂTÉ DI MELANZANA

EGGPLANT SPREAD

FOR 8 PEOPLE

❉

BOTH BECAUSE THE EGGPLANT REDUCES DRAMATICALLY IN COOKING AND THE OTHER INGREDIENTS HAVE A RESOLUTELY ZESTY NATURE, A LITTLE OF THIS MOUTH-WATERING SPREAD GOES A LONG WAY ON *crostini*.

❉ *1 large eggplant (about 1-½ pounds), peeled and cut into 1-inch dice*
❉ *salt*
❉ *3 tablespoons extra-virgin olive oil*
❉ *3 cloves garlic, finely chopped*
❉ *1 small onion, chopped*
❉ *1 tablespoon drained small capers or coarsely chopped large capers*
❉ *1 tablespoon chopped fresh Italian parsley*
❉ *2 anchovy fillets in olive oil, drained*
❉ *freshly milled black pepper*
❉ *1 recipe Toasts (see page 123)*

❶ PLACE THE EGGPLANT in a colander placed in the sink over a bowl. Sprinkle it with salt and let stand so that the bitter liquor from the seeds runs out, about 40 minutes. Rinse under fresh water and dry well with a cotton kitchen towel.

❷ IN A FRYING PAN over medium heat, warm the olive oil. Add the garlic and onion and sauté gently until softened but not browned, about 5 minutes. Add the eggplant cubes and stir to coat all the pieces. Cover and cook gently, stirring occasionally to prevent sticking, until the eggplant is very soft, about 10 minutes. Remove the pan from the heat and stir in the capers and parsley.

❸ IN A SMALL DISH, mash the anchovies to a paste. Add to the eggplant and mix thoroughly. Season to taste with salt and pepper. Spread the eggplant on the *crostini* and serve.

VARIATION: Increase the olive oil by 1 tablespoon. Add ¼ pound fresh white cultivated mushrooms, cleaned and sliced, to the pan when adding the eggplant.

BURRI COMPOSTI
FLAVORED BUTTERS

In *Il Talismano della felicitá*, the bible of Italian cooking first published in the 1920s, Ada Boni gives nearly twenty suggestions for these flavored butters that are frequently used for canapés, in *panini* (bunlike sandwiches), *tramezzini* (page 121), and *crostini*. Here are a few that I have used regularly, but certainly other ingredients can be pounded with butter and whipped. Other possibilities include various fresh herbs, cooked shrimp and lobster, sardines, and many types of smoked fish.

Burro di tonno
Tuna Butter

* *½ pound unsalted butter, at room temperature*
* *1 can (6 ounces) imported Italian light tuna in olive oil, drained*
* *⅓ cup drained small capers*

In a food processor fitted with the metal blade, blend together the butter and tuna until perfectly smooth. Spread on warm (not hot) *crostini.* Garnish each *crostino* with a few capers.

Burro di gorgonzola
Gorgonzola Butter

* *6 tablespoons unsalted butter, at room temperature*
* *¾ pound mild (young) gorgonzola*
* *parmigiano shavings (optional)*

In a food processor fitted with the metal blade, blend together the butter and *gorgonzola* until perfectly smooth. Spread on warm (not hot) *crostini.* Garnish each *crostino* with shavings of *parmigiano,* if desired.

Burro di caviale
Caviar Butter

* *¼ pound unsalted butter, at room temperature*
* *¼ pound red caviar*

In a bowl combine the butter and caviar. Using a wooden spoon, stir until a smooth, even mixture forms; take care not to purée the caviar completely. Spread on warm (not hot) *crostini.*

Burro di salmone affumicato
Smoked Salmon Butter

* *¼ pound unsalted butter, at room temperature*
* *3 ounces smoked salmon*
* *fresh tarragon leaves (optional)*

In a food processor fitted with the metal blade, blend together the butter and salmon until perfectly smooth. Spread on warm (not hot) *crostini.* Garnish each *crostino* with tarragon, if desired.

Burro d'acciuga
Anchovy Butter

* *¼ pound unsalted butter, at room temperature*
* *4 anchovy fillets in olive oil, drained*

In a food processor fitted with the metal blade, blend together the butter and anchovies until perfectly smooth. Spread on warm (not hot) *crostini.*

SALSA VERDE

GREEN SAUCE

MAKES ABOUT ¾ CUP

❋

THERE ARE MANY VARIATIONS ON *salsa verde*, THE CLASSIC ITALIAN SAUCE WITHOUT WHICH THE FAMOUS *bollito misto*, AN ELEGANT BOILED DINNER OF BEEF, VEAL, CAPON, *cotechino* (FINE ITALIAN PORK SAUSAGE), AND OTHER MEAT DELICACIES WOULD BE UNTHINKABLE. WHEN SERVING THIS SAUCE WITH SLICED HOT OR COLD BOILED BEEF FOR AN *antipasto*, I ADD A TEASPOON OR SO OF DIJON-STYLE MUSTARD AND TWO OR THREE TABLESPOONS OF CHOPPED CORNICHONS. WHEN DRIZZLING *salsa verde* ON POACHED DEBONED CHICKEN FOR AN *antipasto*, I LIKE TO ADD SEVERAL FINELY CHOPPED DRAINED ANCHOVY FILLETS TO COMPENSATE FOR THE FOWL'S BLANDNESS. THE BASIC *salsa verde* THAT FOLLOWS IS THE ONE I ALWAYS BRUSH ONTO DELICATE WHOLE POACHED FISH FOR A TRULY ELEGANT *antipasto*. PITTED AND CHOPPED, SHARPLY FLAVORED GREEN OLIVES ARE AN ASSET TO THE SAUCE WHEN IT IS SERVED WITH FISH OR FOWL.

❋ *½ cup extra-virgin olive oil*
❋ *¼ cup freshly squeezed lemon juice*
❋ *2 teaspoons drained small capers*
❋ *¼ cup chopped fresh Italian parsley leaves*
❋ *2 teaspoons finely chopped green onion*
❋ *1 small clove garlic, finely chopped*
❋ *salt and freshly milled black pepper*

❶ IN A BOWL, stir together all the ingredients, including salt and pepper to taste. Cover and set aside at room temperature until ready to use. Avoid refrigerating it. The sauce is best when used within several hours of making it.

SALSA DI POMODORO AL BASILICO

SIEVED TOMATO SAUCE WITH BASIL

MAKES ABOUT 2 CUPS

❋

IN THIS RECIPE, PLUM TOMATOES (FRESH OR CANNED) ARE SIMMERED SLOWLY WITHOUT SALT, OIL, GARLIC, OR ONION, TO KEEP THEIR NATURAL FLAVOR INTACT. IF USING FRESH TOMATOES, THEY SHOULD BE VERY RIPE, FLESHY, AND SWEET PLUM TOMATOES. IF USING CANNED TOMATOES, USE IMPORTED ITALIAN PLUM TOMATOES, WHICH ARE SWEETER AND MORE FLESHY THAN MOST DOMESTIC VARIETIES (REDPACK BRAND IS AN EXCEPTION). THE SKIN IS LEFT ON THE TOMATOES TO IMPART ADDITIONAL TASTE AND BODY TO THE SAUCE. THE CARROT IS ADDED IN PLACE OF SUGAR TO COMPENSATE FOR EXCESS ACIDITY IN THE TOMATOES. EXTRA-VIRGIN OLIVE OIL IS MIXED IN *after* THE SAUCE IS COOKED SO THAT ITS RAW, FRUITY FLAVOR COMES THROUGH CLEARLY. ❋ THIS SAUCE IS ENORMOUSLY VERSATILE ON THE *antipasto* TABLE WHEN A TOMATO SAUCE IS REQUIRED TO ADD MOISTURE AND FLAVOR AND A HEAVIER SAUCE WOULD OVERWHELM. IT IS JUST THE RIGHT *salsa* ON WHICH TO LAY COLD MEATLOAF (*polpettone*) SLICES, OR WITH WHICH TO ANOINT BAKED STUFFED VEGETABLES. I ALSO LIKE TO USE IT ON THIN DRIED PASTA SUCH AS *spaghettini* AND *capellini* BECAUSE ITS LIGHT, SIEVED TEXTURE MARRIES WELL WITH SUCH DELICATE CUTS. BUT IT GOES WELL WITH JUST ABOUT ALL PASTA CUTS, AS WELL AS WITH HOMEMADE FRESH POTATO *gnocchi*.

* *2-½ pounds fresh vine-ripened plum tomatoes, cut into quarters, or 1 can (28 ounces) plum tomatoes in purée, cut into quarters*
* *1 small carrot, peeled and quartered*
* *¼ teaspoon salt, or to taste*
* *freshly milled black pepper*
* *2 to 3 tablespoons extra-virgin olive oil, or to taste*
* *3 tablespoons finely torn fresh basil*

❶ PUT THE FRESH TOMATOES or the canned tomatoes in purée and the carrot in a saucepan. Cook, uncovered, over gentle heat, stirring occasionally, until thickened, about 40 minutes. If you see that the tomatoes contain a great deal of water, drain off excess liquid as the tomatoes cook.

❷ STRAIN THE TOMATOES through a food mill, pressing to get as much of the pulp as you can through the fine holes. (This really must be done in a food mill in order to restrain the skins and seeds while finely puréeing the tomatoes; avoid puréeing in the food processor because it will not restrain the peels and seeds.) If the sauce is too thin (this will depend on the texture and water content of the tomatoes), return it to the saucepan and simmer for up to 20 minutes longer. Season with salt, pepper to taste, olive oil, and basil.

VARIATION: Fresh mint leaves can be substituted for the basil.

SALSA ROSSA CRUDA

UNCOOKED TOMATO SAUCE

MAKES ABOUT 1-½ CUPS

❋

THIS IS A SAUCE WITH MANY USES. IT IS A CLASSIC ACCOMPANIMENT TO BOILED MEATS AND FOWL; IF SLICED BLACK OLIVES ARE ADDED, IT IS A FINE COMPANION TO POACHED FISH DISHES SUCH AS IN A DELICIOUS COLD LIGURIAN *antipasto* OF POACHED ROLLED SOLE FILLETS. A POPULAR USE FOR *salsa rossa cruda* IS AS A TOPPING FOR *bruschetta,* THE ITALIAN TOAST RUBBED WITH GARLIC AND DRIZZLED WITH OLIVE OIL DISCUSSED ON PAGE XX. FOR A LITTLE MORE ZEST, ADD SOME BALSAMIC VINE-GAR. TO SERVE IT WITH MEATS, THE TUSCANS SOMETIMES ADD LIGHTLY TOASTED DRIED BREAD CRUMBS AND CHOPPED PARSLEY. IT IS ALSO THE BASE FOR AN UNCOOKED SUMMER PASTA SAUCE, TO WHICH CAPERS AND GOOD SHARP OLIVES ARE ADDED. ❋ IT IS IMPOSSIBLE TO MAKE THIS LOVELY SAUCE WITHOUT SWEET, VINE-RIPENED TOMATOES. THE IDEAL TOMATO IS A FRESH ITALIAN PLUM TOMATO, BUT THESE ARE NOT SO EASY TO COME BY IN AMERICA. THE NEXT BEST ARE TASTY VINE-RIPENED TOMATOES, POSSIBLE TO FIND DURING THE SUMMER WHEN FARM STANDS SELL FRESH PRODUCE. GOOD CANNED PLUM TOMATOES ARE ACTUALLY PREFERABLE TO THE TASTELESS SUPERMARKET VARIETY. CHERRY TOMATOES ARE OFTEN SWEET AND TASTY, AND WIDELY AVAILABLE, ALTHOUGH THEY REQUIRE A LITTLE MORE WORK TO PEEL AND SEED THAN OTHER TOMATOES.

✳ *1 small clove garlic, finely chopped or passed through a garlic press*

✳ *1-½ pounds fresh vine-ripened plum toma-toes, or 1-½ cups well-drained canned plum tomatoes*

✳ *¼ cup torn or chopped fresh basil*

✳ *¼ cup extra-virgin olive oil*

✳ *½ teaspoon salt, or to taste*

✳ *freshly milled black pepper*

❶ IF USING FRESH TOMATOES, bring a large saucepan filled with water to a boil. Add the tomatoes, blanch for less than 30 seconds, drain, and immediately plunge them into cold water. Remove the skins and seeds and chop the tomatoes. If using canned tomatoes, remove their seeds, squeeze out excess liquid, and chop them.

❷ IN A BOWL, mix together the tomatoes and all the other ingredients, including pepper to taste. Let stand for 1 to 3 hours before using.

AHEAD-OF-TIME NOTE: This sauce can be made 1 to 2 days in advance, covered, and refrigerated.

MAIL-ORDER SOURCES
FOR ITALIAN COOKING EQUIPMENT & PROVISIONS

AMERICAN SPOON FOODS
P.O. Box 566
Petoskey, Michigan 49770
616 347-9030, 800 222-5886
Stocks dried morels, porcini, *and shiitakes.*

AUX DELICES DES BOIS, INC.
4 Leonard Street
New York, New York 10013
212 334-1230
Stocks all types of cultivated and imported mushrooms; sun-dried tomatoes. Will accept phone orders for overnight delivery.

DEAN & DELUCA
Mail-Order Department
560 Broadway
New York, New York 10012
212 431-1691, 800 221-7714, ext. 223 or 270
Kitchen equipment; Italian specialty foods, imported dried mushrooms, cured meats and preserved fish.
✳ Catalog available.

G. B. RATTO INTERNATIONAL GROCER
821 Washington Street
Oakland, California 94607
800 228-3515 (California)
800 325-3483 (out of state)
Italian specialty foods, imported dried mushrooms, cured meats and preserved fish; large assortment of grains, flours, herbs, and spices.
✳ Catalog available.

HANS JOHANSSON
44 West 74th Street
New York, New York 10023
212 787-6496
Stocks dried morels, cèpes, porcini, *black trumpets,* chanterelles, *and* shiitakes.

MANGANARO FOODS
488 Ninth Avenue
New York, New York 10018
212 563-5331, 800 472-5264
Italian specialty foods, imported dried mushrooms.
✳ Catalog available.

METRO AGRI BUSINESS
47 Wooster Street
New York, New York 10013
212 431-3504
Stocks dried porcini *and morels.*

THE MOZZARELLA COMPANY
2944 Elm Street
Dallas, Texas 75226
214 741-4072, 800 798-2954
Large variety of fresh and aged cheeses; sun-dried tomatoes; imported olive oils and balsamic vinegar.
Cheeses shipped overnight.

THE SANDY MUSH HERB NURSERY
Route 2, Surrett Cove Road
Leicester, North Carolina 28748
704 683-2014
Live herbs and herb seeds shipped. Lovely illustrated catalog ($4, refundable with first order) includes suggested herb-garden patterns, information about growing and drying herbs, recipes.

TODARO BROTHERS
555 Second Avenue
New York, New York 10016
212 679-7766
Italian specialty foods, good selection of cured meats and imported cheeses.
✳ Catalog available.

WILLIAMS-SONOMA
Mail-Order Department
P.O. Box 7456
San Francisco, California 94120-7456
415 421-4242, 800 541-2233
Kitchen equipment; some Italian specialty foods.
✳ Catalog available.

W. J. CLARK & CO.
5400 West Roosevelt Road
Chicago, Illinois 60650
312 626-3676, 800 229-0090
Stocks dried porcini, shiitakes, *morels, and oyster mushrooms; chopped and powdered dried wild mushrooms.*
✳ Free catalog available.

ZABAR'S
Mail-Order Department
2245 Broadway
New York, New York 10024
212 787-2003, 800 221-3347
Kitchen equipment; some Italian specialty foods, cured meats and preserved fish, imported cheeses.
✳ Catalog available.

INDEX

TABLE OF EQUIVALENTS

THE EXACT EQUIVALENTS IN THE FOLLOWING TABLES HAVE
BEEN ROUNDED FOR CONVENIENCE

❋

US/UK

oz = ounce
lb = pound
in = inch
ft = foot
tbl = tablespoon
fl oz = fluid ounce
qt = quart

METRIC

g = gram
kg = kilogram
mm = millimeter
cm = centimeter
ml = milliliter
l = liter

WEIGHTS

US/UK	Metric
1 oz	30 g
2 oz	60 g
3 oz	90 g
4 oz (¼ lb)	125 g
5 oz (⅓ lb)	155 g
6 oz	185 g
7 oz	220 g
8 oz (½ lb)	250 g
10 oz	315 g
12 oz (¾ lb)	375 g
14 oz	440 g
16 oz (1 lb)	500 g
1½ lb	750 g
2 lb	1 kg
3 lb	1.5 kg

OVEN TEMPERATURES

Fahrenheit	Celsius	Gas
250	120	½
275	140	1
300	150	2
325	160	3
350	180	4
375	190	5
400	200	6
425	220	7
450	230	8
475	240	9
500	260	10

LENGTH MEASURES

⅛ in	3 mm
¼ in	6 mm
½ in	12 mm
1 in	2.5 cm
2 in	5 cm
3 in	7.5 cm
4 in	10 cm
5 in	13 cm
6 in	15 cm
7 in	18 cm
8 in	20 cm
9 in	23 cm
10 in	25 cm
11 in	28 cm
12 in/1 ft	30 cm

LIQUIDS

US	Metric	UK
2 tbl	30 ml	1 fl oz
¼ cup	60 ml	2 fl oz
⅓ cup	80 ml	3 fl oz
½ cup	125 ml	4 fl oz
⅔ cup	160 ml	5 fl oz
¾ cup	180 ml	6 fl oz
1 cup	250 ml	8 fl oz
1½ cups	375 ml	12 fl oz
2 cups	500 ml	16 fl oz
4 cups/1 qt	1 l	32 fl oz

EQUIVALENTS FOR COMMONLY
USED INGREDIENTS

❀

BROWN SUGAR

¼ cup	1½ oz	45 g
½ cup	3 oz	90 g
¾ cup	4 oz	125 g
1 cup	5½ oz	170 g
1½ cups	8 oz	250 g
2 cups	10 oz	315 g

WHITE SUGAR

¼ cup	2 oz	60 g
⅓ cup	3 oz	90 g
½ cup	4 oz	125 g
¾ cup	6 oz	185 g
1 cup	8 oz	250 g
1½ cups	12 oz	375 g
2 cups	1 lb	500 g

DRIED BEANS

¼ cup	1½ oz	45 g
⅓ cup	2 oz	60 g
½ cup	3 oz	90 g
¾ cup	5 oz	155 g
1 cup	6 oz	185 g
1¼ cups	8 oz	250 g
1½ cups	12 oz	375 g

ROLLED OATS

⅓ cup	1 oz	30 g
⅔ cup	2 oz	60 g
1 cup	3 oz	90 g
1½ cups	4 oz	125 g
2 cups	5 oz	155 g

JAM, HONEY

2 tbl	2 oz	60 g
¼ cup	3 oz	90g
½ cup	5 oz	155 g
¾ cup	8 oz	250 g
1 cup	11 oz	345 g

ALL-PURPOSE (PLAIN) FLOUR, DRIED BREAD CRUMBS, CHOPPED NUTS

¼ cup	1 oz	30g
⅓ cup	1½ oz	45 g
½ cup	2 oz	60 g
¾ cup	3 oz	90 g
1 cup	4 oz	125 g
1½ cups	6 oz	185 g
2 cups	8 oz	250 g

WHOLE-WHEAT (WHOLEMEAL) FLOUR

3 tbl	1 oz	30 g
½ cup	2 oz	60 g
⅔ cup	3 oz	90 g
1 cup	4 oz	125 g
1¼ cups	5 oz	155 g
1⅔ cups	7 oz	210 g
1¾ cups	8 oz	250 g

LONG-GRAIN RICE, CORNMEAL

⅓ cup	2 oz	60 g
½ cup	2½ oz	75 g
¾ cup	4 oz	125 g
1 cup	5 oz	155 g
1½ cups	8 oz	250 g

GRATED PARMESAN, ROMANO CHEESE

¼ cup	1 oz	30 g
½ cup	2 oz	60 g
¾ cup	3 oz	90 g
1 cup	4 oz	125 g
1⅓ cups	5 oz	155 g
2 cups	7 oz	210 g

RAISINS, CURRANTS, SEMOLINA

¼ cup	1 oz	30 g
⅓ cup	2 oz	60 g
½ cup	3 oz	90 g
¾ cup	4 oz	125 g
1 cup	5 oz	155 g